C000139576

Against Art

SEAGULL WORLD LITERATURE

Against Art

(THE NOTEBOOKS)

TOMAS ESPEDAL

TRANSLATED BY JAMES ANDERSON

LONDON NEW YORK CALCUTTA

Seagull Books, 2011

Imot Kunsten: notatbøkene

© Gyldendal Norsk Forlag AS 2009. [All rights reserved.]

English translation © James Anderson, 2010

This translation has been published
with the financial support of NORLA

First published in English by Seagull Books, 2011

ISBN 13   978 0 8574 2 018 3

British Library Cataloguing-in-Publication Data
A catalogue record for this book is available
from the British Library

Typeset by Seagull Books, Calcutta, India
Printed and bound in India by Hyam Enterprises,
Calcutta, India

To my mother

APRIL

To remain: this is something
that also needs courage.

Kristian Lundberg

My first name was made in a factory, cast in metal, and had a certain permanence. I have tried to forget it. I'm forty-three—forty-four—forty-five—forty-six years old. I write this in September. I was born on 12 November in the sign of Scorpio. I've been told that when a scorpion is threatened, when it's cornered and can't escape, it raises its sting and forces it between the two carapaces that protect its body; the poison is pumped in. Spring, autumn is the season I like most of all, the summer is past, I can begin working, November, September, the ninth or the nineteenth, the twenty-ninth; I start writing in the morning or in the evening. The house is quiet. I'm not frightened or backed into a corner, I raise my right hand and place the pencil point on the paper, the poison is pumped out. I write. That first sentence, like pressing a needle to the skin, a slight resistance, soft and the needle enters, it passes through and finds the artery; it is necessary to forget. My other name was more difficult, softer, harder, a woman's name. It took me a long time to destroy it. Not because it was invincible, but because it was old, it was linked to a place; I've never been there.

I was born in a city, the name comes from the outskirts, a dry, wind-blown and unyielding name, it snapped like some stubborn tree. That first sentence must be as hard as steel. You work it up, hone and polish, chip and refine, a piece of craftsmanship. The mechanical clatter of the typewriter, like sitting alone in a factory hearing the voices of people who aren't there; idle hands and heavy boots that tramp across the floor without making a sound. The sentence gleams. Hard as steel. My daughter and I have something in common, we both lost our mothers. I lost my mother in April, she lost her mother in September. I didn't know what to say, how I could comfort her, all I managed to say, the first thing I said, as if I were a child, as if no years could separate us, as if I wanted her to console me and for us to embrace one another in a common grief, two soulmates, of the same age, as if I in the course of a few wordless minutes had turned her into an adult, my future partner in life, my hope; she heard it and turned away, angry and afraid, it was no solace, the first thing I said was: We have no mother.

My daughter is fifteen and doesn't know her father. He's a man who writes books, you might say, and quite a different man from her father. I've tried my best, after she lost her mother, to be a good father to her. I also tried to be a sort of mother, it was a big mistake which I plunged into with all my energy and a steadfast will; I stopped writing, stopped travelling, terminated some friendships and installed myself in our new home like a mother. I seldom left the house. Stayed at home, washed and tidied, constantly cleaned the rooms and the sheets and her clothes. I cooked dinner and breakfast and made up the lunchbox she took with her to school. Always regular meals. Always clean clothes. Always someone at home, morning and evening. I enjoyed it a lot, more than I would have believed; I loved going shopping and making food, tidying, washing clothes, hanging them out to dry, it did me good. But my child wasn't happy, she missed not only her mother but also her father. One day she said: Why are you always at home? Why can't you leave me in peace, alone for one day, on my own, why can't you get out of the house?

I went into town.

Reluctantly I went into town, what did I want there?

I walked the streets and whiled the time away, two, three, four hours and then I went home. I wanted to be at home with my daughter. She needed a father and she'd got a grief-stricken man, who thought he'd lose his reason, go mad, who thought he would die, become ill, who thought he'd lose everything, his house, his child, he was convinced something terrible would happen. He was waiting for it, but the terrible thing didn't happen, not in our household. Our neighbour suffered a massive heart attack and collapsed outside his house. The nest in the tree in the garden was attacked by a bird of prey which pulled it out of the tree and cracked open the eggs, ate the young and flew away. Terrible things were happening, all the time, everywhere, except in our house. Our house was sacred, a peace lay over it. And in this peace, in this waiting time I began to write. Each morning, after my daughter had left for school, I sat down at my writing table. A dull, white silence enveloped the house. It frightened me, I wasn't used to the silence, I'd washed and swept it away while I'd waited for the terrible thing, but now that the silence was here, it came as a sudden and unexpected joy. The silence took up residence in the house, and after a few weeks it had become part of me too, it had entered what I was writing.

Like snow. A white, dull snow after a long summer and a warm autumn. Wind, rain and suddenly snow, the first snow. The crows hop across the garden from left to right making words in the snow; small, black scribblings, messily written, the birds are writing, so quickly and precisely, they're writing: Winter is coming.

The roses stiffen.

White and covered with frost.

They never even withered, standing as if arrested in death, hard frozen and tied up to the white house wall with lengths of red wool: bound, arrested, forced to stand like icy mouths so open in the darkness.

Mist in the morning. It evaporates, hangs there like remnant splashes of water in the rose petals' furls, wet hair tied back in a ponytail and held with one hand so hard that you scream to the silence outside: Come. Winter comes, too early again, and the snow melts, the mist lifts, sunlight breaks through the white canopy of leaves and touches the frozen rose petals which close too late and wither.

Flowers tied up with wool from your red jumper.

White climbing roses.

In the garden.

In front of the house, tied to the white cladding with red wool fixed to the wall with drawing pins and looped around the flower stalks so as to force the white roses up towards the window where I sit and write.

Tied.

Tied to the house and the rooms where I'm also bound to the bed on which I lie and the chair on which I sit. I move round the house on an extending lead, with no desire to leave or break loose. Instead I work at tightening the invisible threads which I prepare and make impervious, thicken and lengthen, so that I can tighten them up and twine them round and round my mouth and neck and chest, round and round, harder and harder, until at last I'm encased in a hard, white cocoon. A protective membrane of threads fixed to the walls and floor, writing table and chair. Here I sit, imprisoned and patient, forced to watch how the thin structure becomes so comprehensive and intricate that it can be called a home.

A home.

This road, ah that road, the gravel road that leads tentatively up to the house and is the same colour as the house because it's a part of the house, an extension of the door, a continuation of something inside; the bed, perhaps, where he lies and doesn't want to get up.

These hours in the middle of the day when you're wide awake and lie on the bed, not to sleep, not to rest, but to look out of the window, at the sky outside, to be even more wide awake. So wide awake that suddenly, in repose, he understands that he could lie like this for ever, motionless and without thoughts, but with a gaze so pure that it hurts. What is it he sees? The sky, the clouds, nothing more. But then he shifts his gaze and sees the walls and the ceiling of the room he's in; the lamp on the writing table by the window, the chair and the red carpet, the books on the bedside table and the notebooks with covers the same colour as the house, and this makes him think about all the things he cannot see, the things he should have described: the gravel road running down from the house, this road on which the trees cast shadows so hard and impassable that he wonders if he'll ever be able to cross them and leave the house.

The letter: 'It's probably true to say that I share Bonnard's taste for the uncomfortable. Simple furniture, hard chairs, spartan rooms, without decoration. They say that the room he worked in had no resting places, no sofa, no furniture. I believe he was too fond of all this to want to own it; he transferred it to his work. His work was to see. Outside the window, in the garden, Marthe lounges in an easy chair. Hair unkempt, a white dressing gown, it is morning or evening. His work was to observe her, he sketched what she did: how she woke in the morning, how she got up and bathed, ate her breakfast, embroidered a tablecloth, wrote a letter. She sits in the garden, the letter lies on the table on the embroidered tablecloth. The light among the fruit trees, cherries in a basket, we could almost eat them. I sit at my writing table and look out; the fruit trees and garden table, the empty easy chair, it is Saturday or Sunday. I'm trying to write, but with no success so am writing this letter instead: I need you.'

I couldn't get to grips with this day, it turned into a totally hopeless day for me, it didn't turn out the way I'd wanted, well, what did I want of this day?

Can I say that I lost it, that I lost the day, how many days have I lost in this manner? It wasn't my day. The day began well, it was a good start to a good day: I left the house, went out of the door, down the gravel road, through the gate and left, heading for the long roundabout route to the shop, and I'd no sooner got on to my usual path, than I could tell this was the start of a good day: clouds above the neighbouring house. Heavy, static clouds of such density and weight that you stopped to look at them. Portentous clouds? If they'd been able to fall with the same weight that they hung in the air, they would have crushed my neighbour's house. But the clouds fell as rain, it was raining. A mild, light rain on my neighbour's roof, it lifted my spirits. The air cleared, the clouds broke, the sun came through; I was on my way to the shop. To the right now, and I was in the clearing among the trees, a clearing in the wood, it's a very definite place. What sort of place? A nowhere place? And yet a place, it's strange. Nothing visible. Nothing audible, either. So, just strange. Strange each and every time I enter that little glade among the trees, the glade in the wood. Here I pause. No more than that, just pause. The same place. Always pause in the same place. A pausing place perhaps? Yesterday I imagined an animal just here. A squirrel, that was it, a fleeing squirrel, it was fleeing from me. Today I saw something quite different at the same spot: a crowd of strangers sitting and lying on the ground. Rugs had been spread out. They sat and lay on the grass; an excursion; I only noticed their clothes, summer clothes, white. No voices, no words, just silence. Later I thought that they must have been dead, that they belonged to a different time; I walked quietly past, and in that instant it was as if I recognized one of the faces, I waved, but there was no answering wave. She didn't recognize me.

It wasn't here I lost the day.

I continued down the path and came to the enclosure where the horses live. They stand in the middle of the paddock, motionless, like statues, almost, then suddenly one of them begins to move: its muscles show, a violent twitching under the smooth skin and the feet thudding hard on the ground, the terrible sound of hooves, like some omen of war, or death. A calamity. Something awful. The horse galloped furiously up to where I stood. I felt no fear. And then: how the wave of air from the creature struck my face. The waft of skin, of horsehair, it struck me in the face. That, too, was a joy.

Was it here the day turned, turned against me? I hadn't lost it yet, walked past the paddock and broke a stick from one of the trees that lay on the ground; the farmer's work, the farmer's warmth and winter, I broke off a stick of the right size: now I was going to pass the dogs. The farmer's dogs, running loose. Four loose dogs, running in a pack. And now I feel the fear; the fear I don't feel for horses I feel for dogs. It does me good. I enjoy this fear. My heart pounds, my hands come alive, my feet, my blood, everything inside me quickens. I'm encircled by dogs. They snarl and snap, nip and tug at the sleeve of my jacket, now I wield my stick. A whistling sound. It's the farmer blowing his whistle, the dogs turn to look, they turn around. I need the dogs, need the fear, but not the farmer: this notion of property. That his property encompasses this entire area of woodland and fields, sea rocks, beach and sea, he behaves as if he owns the whole of this part of the island. This is what I can't bear. And on this day of all days, on my day, I walked straight up to him, a short, heavy man with a hard face, ruddy and red. I wagged my finger under his nose. Dogs must be kept on a leash everywhere on this island, I said. This is my route to the shop. This is my route to the sea. I'll swim when I like, where I like, and this spring, this summer in particular, I said, my last summer on the island, I've no intention of being harassed or hindered, not by you or your dogs.

Had I planned to move? This surprised me. The thought hadn't even dawned before I was suddenly saying: My last summer on the island. Where did this notion come from? Where was I moving to? I was tied to the house and my daughter; she went to school here, had friends here, was secure here, wasn't that also my salvation, my good fortune, that I couldn't

choose, that I was tied to her and the house and my
work here? So where had I got this idea of moving
from? I stood in front of the man who for several
years had weekly, daily, disturbed my walk to the shop.
The dogs, the whistles, the insults and threats, enough
was enough. I needed the fear, but anger did me no
good, you get caught up in it, like when your jacket
gets caught on a barbed-wire fence. You get caught
up in your own rage. I abused him, threatened him, it
was a big mistake, now my walk would never be the
same again, it would be different. I stood there ruining one of the finest moments I had, the walk to the
shop. He turned on his heel, went into the house,
reappeared with a shotgun, he held it low, but his
voice had a particular confidence in it: For the last
time, this is my land you're crossing.

I was in the process of losing the day. My anger
remained with me, long after I'd torn myself away
from the landowner. I walked furiously towards the
shop. Tried to glimpse something that might please
me; the white anemones, they grew in white circles
between the birch trunks; I didn't see them. The daffodils in ranks of yellow, white where once there'd
been greenhouses; the greenhouses had gone, but the

daffodils remained, they grew wild in large patches among the trees, a stunning sight, every time; usually I stopped, but now I walked past. A special apple tree in the garden in front of the red house, the white apple blossom, a sharp, white beauty, as if these small, bright blooms sliced the air, or sliced the breath, you noticed them slicing your breath; the stinging certainty that these white flowers would turn into apples. Had I lifted my gaze, I'd have seen how the magpies were building their nests: twig on twig, painstakingly made, woven and made basket-shaped with a lining of grass, grass and earth, cemented with water, small master-builders of birds; here they would lay their eggs, white and grey, as if the outside of the shell was an intimation of the chicks' plumage; their lack of colour.

The sky's blue. The rhododendron's red. The chrysanthemum's yellow.

I saw nothing of this.

I lost the day, did this mean that I lost sight of it?

The birds, the colours, the possibilities, the pleasures; I couldn't see them; I'd lost one of my best routines, the walk to the shop, and with it I'd lost the day, presumably tomorrow too and several other days besides, yes, my entire future on the island. I must find a new route to walk, a new custom, if not my time on the island is at an end: I'll have to move.

Was that really all it took to blight this day of mine, my entire future: the disruption of one of my habits? Yes, it took no more to knock me off balance and propel me into the darkness, for one sombre moment all was black. For one sombre moment it was as if I'd lost everything: the day, my vision, my courage, my will; the only desire I had was the desire to give up.

For one sombre moment it was all over; I'd lost my beginning.

I was on the way to the shop, I saw nothing. No trees, no road, no freedom, no future, nothing.

And so it was a fragile thing, this day of mine; I'd have to build it on surer ground, a deeper necessity, perhaps everything would have to be rearranged, all my habits exchanged for new ones? Or even more difficult: to do without habits at all?

Or, I'd have to teach myself to see: to see the same things with new eyes. Moving alters nothing. To move is to postpone repetition. To remain, another summer, one more spring, in the same place, in the same house, that would change everything.

One morning I awoke and couldn't recognize the room I was in; I assumed I was spending the night with a friend, or perhaps in a hotel, the bed was by the open window; I was at Janne's in town. It was quiet in the room, cold, no traffic, no breathing or warmth from a body next to mine; I was alone in the bed. So I must be in the bedroom at Dreggen. Had I moved the bed into the living room at last, nearer to the veranda door, so that I could sleep with the door open, with a view of the mountains and the sea, and not of the backyard? No, that had never materialized. I'd never got around to it. I'd moved, had had to move as quickly as possible; I was sleeping in the house at Askøy. Soon the girls would wake, first the younger, then the elder, then their mother, always in that order, I couldn't hear them yet. Surely, their mother would get up soon? It took me a little while to recall that she was ill, that she was dead, that Harriet had moved out, that I lived alone with Amalie. Where was she? I couldn't hear her, had she left too? How old was she now? Was it all over already; the light came in from the window high in the wall, I couldn't move my arms, or my legs, how long had I been lying like this? Now I remembered, when I'd fallen asleep she'd been fifteen, she'd been going to a party; how she'd made herself up, a grown girl, almost. I'd slept in the living room to wait for her, to hear her get home, in through the front door at night, just a child. And for a few seconds I couldn't recognize the room I was in, it was enough to make me lose both name and age.

My first name was Olsen. Alfred Johan Olsen was a squat, stocky man with a friendly face, people said, a gloomy and candid face, my grandmother Elly Alice said, and, she noticed, strong hands; they first met at a cabin which a group of workmates had built in the forest under the peak of Løvstakken. He worked at the Solheimsviken shipyard, he'd taken the name Olsen when he moved to the city. His family was Fjøsanger, he was the youngest of eight, and as the name suggests he came from a farm quite close to the city they could now see across from the cabin where they played cards and smoked their pipes. They'd noticed two young girls walking arm in arm each evening, with seeming nonchalance, past the cabin.

One evening the companions summoned their courage and called the two girls in. They were sisters, Margit and Elly Alice, nineteen and seventeen years old. The younger was the prettier. She stood in the doorway hesitant to enter. Margit had already seated herself on a chair, she did the talking, she said that they lived with their father who was on his own. He'd lost his wife when the girls were young. Now he'd met a younger woman, Thea, she was only a year or two older than Margit, Elly Alice told me.

One evening the woman called Thea came to the house and knocked at the door: Is Espedal in? she asked. He's resting, said Elly, she could see at once that the girl was pregnant. Reluctantly, Elly went to the parlour, her father lay on the sofa, tired after a long day on the railway. She tried to wake him, he opened one irritated eye. There's a girl at the door, she's asking for Espedal, said Elly. Damn, said her father; damn, he said again. My grandmother liked telling this story, it was like tearing the scab off a wound and making it bleed all over again, she scratched nervously at her arm and repeated the same thing over and over; damn, he said, damn, she said. Thea moved in and made it plain that the two girls must move out. Thea's mother came on a visit, the girls lay in their bedroom listening to the two women talking: How could you, the mother said. An older man with two grown girls, how could you? What were you thinking of? Poor little Thea. I'll get them out of the house, Thea said. The girls heard that. Margit leapt out of bed and ran into the parlour and slapped Thea's face. As hard as she could with the flat of her hand. The two of them fought, well matched, the same age, they let fly and pulled each other's hair. They spat at each other. Kicked and clawed. Margit came back, weeping, to the girls' bedroom, the two sisters lay clutching one another; a few weeks later Margit had to move out. One evening after the sisters had taken their usual walk past the cabin in the woods, Elly Alice found the door locked when she got home, her father was out, and she had to lie down on the front steps to sleep. Eivind Espedal found his daughter sleeping outside the house. The house in which he'd lost his wife, the house his elder daughter had quit in rage and despair, and now here was his favourite daughter asleep on the step, she'd curled up under her coat which she pulled round herself as if for protection. Just at this point in the story I had to get up from the table where we sat in the kitchen of the small third floor flat in Michael Krohnsgate, where my grandmother had lived all her adult life; two small rooms, one had served as a bedroom for a family of three, the other contained a dining table and a fireplace, simple furniture, spartan rooms, unadorned. A kitchen, cold water, hot water and bath in the basement, it was still the same, she had to heat water on an electric ring. We were having breakfast. Every Friday I would walk from Bjørnsonsgate down to Danmarksplass, down beneath the traffic and bear left in the subway, left towards Solheimsviken and Michael Krohnsgate, past the disused shipyards and the brick dwellings that climbed the hillside in terraces and streets on the sunless side of the Laksevåg road, I'd stroll up the pavement toward the Puddefjord bridge to have breakfast with her, every Friday, Elly Alice Espedal, my paternal grandmother, would spread an oilcloth on the kitchen table, a couple of large Sunday plates, her thin coffee cups, Russian, hand-painted: St Petersburg, butter knives from England, Sheffield, the steelworks there, she'd never been anywhere, never been abroad, just to and from work, back and forth between husband and child, home and family, kitchen and bedroom, these were her places, this was her place: the kitchen, the kitchen table, the window on to the harbour. The view of the sea. The freighters that glided to and fro across the kitchen windowpane. We'd have breakfast and smoke cigarettes. I'd loved her, I loved her still. She was beautiful, a keen, wrinkled face with chinks of blue eyes and a full mouth from which the creases in her skin ran in lines sewing her face and mouth together in a disturbing beauty, she had a dangerous face. The grey curls grew in a wild wreath of hair round her face. Grew unrestrained and curled round her forehead and fell into her eyes and into her mouth when she was speaking. She could say anything, it wasn't easy to follow, her stream of words, she jumped backwards and forwards in time, what I mean is, tenses didn't exist for her, everything she narrated was mixed into one tense, here and now, in the kitchen in Michael Krohnsgate. What she was speaking of happened today, she called me Eivind and Alfred, and suddenly she would realize I was neither of them, that it was long ago that she'd lain outside the house and slept on the steps, shut out, she stopped suddenly in her story, stared at me as if I were a stranger: Who was I? Where was she? What house was this, what age was she, a moment ago she'd been seventeen, now she was seventy-eight, it took a moment for her to collect herself, before she was able to relocate the flat and the kitchen in which she sat, and then she stared desperately at the man on the other side of the kitchen table: I've always loved you, she said. I had to leave the table and go out into the little lobby to choke back my tears: it was the image of the young girl sleeping on the steps outside the house, I couldn't understand why it made such an impression on me. I had no daughter then, and I wasn't to know that I'd end up in the same situation as my great-grandfather.

Elly Alice Espedal married Alfred Johan Olsen. She was nineteen, pregnant, they moved into the flat in Michael Krohnsgate. She gave birth to a son, named him Eivind after her father, tried to focus her love in one name. Eivind. Eivind. No wind in the name, no sea, no troubling element, just love and quietness, she wanted it that way; a quiet name, a secure and quiet name, sometimes she would shout the name as loudly as she could.

That first name was love. The second name was necessity, wedlock, work. The second name was hard.

Alfred Johan Olsen worked morning and night, long days, hard toiling days, day shift and evening shift, eight hours a day, Sundays off, a week's holiday in summer, overworked, low wages, exploited, poorly paid; he vanished in his work, vanished from her sight. He was a working man.

When he wasn't working, he missed his work.

When he was at home he had to rest. He rose early, went to bed early. He slept in the dining room, she slept in the large bed with the child, wouldn't, mustn't disturb him. He didn't want to disturb them, mother and child, they were sleeping when he stirred in the morning, at half past five, he went quietly out to the kitchen, put on his working clothes, went down to the cellar to fetch coal. Shovelled the coke into the stove, breathed life into the embers and produced fire, a weak, blue flame. There was snow in the streets and on the rooftops, frost on the windows. In the small flat it was cold and damp. He lit a cigarette. Blew the smoke out of the kitchen window. Boiled water for coffee and had breakfast. Sat on at the kitchen table staring out of the window, the darkness and the cold. The street lamps being lit. These minutes alone in the morning. He loved them; I think he loved them, the minutes and the silence. Then the street lamps were lit. He got up and went out of the door, down the stairs, quietly, imperceptibly, as if silence was his nature, his absence, he crossed the street.

He could hear the bells warning that the shipyard gates were closing and the work beginning. He followed the stream of men that flowed through the gates. They made for the changing rooms and the time-clocks: 06.27, always the same to the minute, he was on the floor of the hall at six-thirty, not a minute before, not a minute after. It wasn't precision so much as a demonstration, he did no more work than necessary, no more, no less. At six-thirty he was at his place by the engines. He built and repaired ships' engines, stood there and welded, screwed and ground, hammered and filed, heavy work and fine work, rough hands and good fingers, his were working hands.

When he was at home, he wasn't at home.

He was distant, tired, ill at ease. He didn't like days off, the long, vacant Sundays. How were they to occupy themselves? In that cramped, cold flat. She wanted to go for a walk. She wanted to visit her father. She took the baby, he carried the pushchair down the stairs and waved them off. He stood watching her back, watching her get smaller and smaller. Only when she'd disappeared, when he could no longer see her back, did he miss her.

She headed for the house in Inndalsveien. A quick walk towards Danmarksplass, up Bjørnsonsgate and into the road she knew so well, the old road home.

The yellow house. The steps outside. The door and the windows; new curtains, a new light from the windows, an alien light in the window, on the first floor, the window looking out over the garden, the apple tree and the fruit bushes, the white climbing roses, the rhododendron and the slender rowan trees which had guarded her and the house; they stood bordering the gravel road that ran past, the protective trees, they hadn't been able to help her. The rowans, red with berries, black with birds, she was among those who walked past now. Who came visiting. She knocked at the door. It was Thea who opened it. Who grudgingly showed them in; Espedal's resting, she said. She showed them into the kitchen. The two women, the mothers, sat on opposite sides of the kitchen table. Thea said nothing, offered nothing, she wanted the other woman to go. Please would you wake my father, said Elly. I want him to see the boy. Thea didn't move. Then I'll go and wake him myself, said Elly. Just you try it, said Thea. He's sleeping with the boy, with Arnfinn, it would be best if you left, she said. Elly Alice jumped up and ran out of the kitchen, through the parlour door and towards the bedroom and the closed door. Thea ran after her, caught a corner of her coat and tried to haul Elly out of the room. She tore the coat off Elly who was pounding on the door, grabbed her hair and pulled it with all her strength, tugged and tore at her hair. Eivind, Elly shouted, she could hear the boy crying in the kitchen. Eivind, Eivind, she screamed.

Do you remember Thea? Elly Alice asked me in the kitchen in Michael Krohnsgate. Yes, of course, I said: every Christmas my father and I drove to Inndalsveien with a present for her; I remembered her as a nice old lady. Well, there you are, said my grandmother, we remember things so differently. Can you remember your great-grandfather? she asked. No, I can't; I've seen photos of him, a big, powerful man perching me on his arm, in the front garden of the house; an image, that's all. How old was I when he died? She considered this and calculated: You might have been two, three or four, she said.

Thea remembered clearly how he walked across the station in his uniform, went out on to the platform and checked the carriages of the long train, tapping the wheels and couplings with a hammer, craning down and forward to shine a torch up at the axles and the underside of the coaches. All was in order. He noted this on his pad. Went forward to the locomotive and climbed into the cab where he noted the kilometres run and the electrical consumption, he wrote down the details and added a general appraisal before signing his name at the bottom of the sheet: Eivind Espedal. Inspector. She stood waiting for him. For him to jump down from the locomotive and walk back along the platform, cross the station quite close to where she and a friend stood. She was wearing her short dress, high heels, a handbag over her shoulder. She had her summer bonnet in her hand, impatiently drumming it against her thigh. Long, dark, curly hair that hung loose to her bare shoulders; there was something Mediterranean about her. She would give him her usual look. He would drop his gaze or return the look; today he looked her right in the eye, a hard and challenging look, it caught her off guard, she felt her heart beat faster and the blood rush to her head, to her face, she turned away. Had he seen it? The way she'd blushed? He was walking quickly, but almost stopped when she turned away, hesitated, before striding towards the office, shut the door, sat down behind the desk and cradled his head in his hands.

Several afternoons a week she stood there, in the same spot, always with a friend. Two young girls, he knew what they wanted, what they were waiting for. Two young girls from the sticks who'd moved to the city, they were on the lookout for a husband. A husband with regular work, a secure job, well paid. Perhaps their mothers had sent them, he thought, had sent their daughters off to the station, almost like prostitutes, off to the railway where they stood flaunting themselves. He'd seen several girls like that, they turned up at the station, more painted and direct than city girls, he'd seen them and he'd passed them by. He lived alone with two girls, two daughters, they didn't need a new mother. He could afford a servant; she tidied and washed and cooked, the two girls liked her, he was content. She did her work and went home, it was a good arrangement. He lived alone, he liked living alone; I believe he liked living alone with his two girls. But from the first moment he saw her, the girl at the station, he took off his wedding ring. It had been more than three years since he'd lost his wife, since she'd died, and yet he hadn't been able to take off the ring, now he took it off, he didn't know why. Was she different? Was there something about her he responded to, a loneliness, sadness, he didn't know what it was; he thought they were alike. He was forty-three years old. She might be nineteen or twenty, perhaps older perhaps younger, he tried not to think about it; her age, his age.

He finished his paperwork. Then he telephoned home. Margit was to take care of Elly Alice, make supper and breakfast, and the packed lunch for school; he wouldn't be home. He had to work over-time. Would spend the night in town. At the railway hotel, the Terminus Hotel, Margit was to telephone there if there was anything important. Thea clearly recalled the way he came walking out of his office, so different, resolute, angry almost, it frightened her, he came walking straight towards her, as if he wanted to chase her, he did want to chase her. She took a quick step backwards, wanted to turn and leave, wanted to run or walk, but he caught hold of her arm, held her fast. That soft voice. So unlike his rugged exterior. She wanted to tear herself away, but his voice held her back, it wasn't what he said, but his voice, that soft, earnest voice. She couldn't remember what he said, perhaps he asked her to walk with him, round the lake, Lungegårdsvann, or in the park; they walked round Lungegårdsvann and in the park, they walked around the town until dusk fell and it had got too dark, he said, for her to go home alone; would she come back to the hotel with him, he had a room there, a service room he called it. She said no, but they went to the hotel together, and then he wanted her to go with him, up to the fifth floor, the room had a balcony and a view of the railway station. The room was large. A large, imposing room with heavy, light-coloured curtains and a chandelier, a dining table and chairs, sofa and occasional table, a whole little living room. A strange man, in a strange room, it was too much for her, it was too soon for her; wasn't he too big for her,

too old, and this room, this recreational home with its
furniture and lamps, did she really want it, wasn't it
being forced on her? What was it her mother had said:
The railway is a good employer, look at the uniforms.
She'd stood at the railway station. She'd looked at the
uniforms. She'd studied the faces, the eyes, she'd made
a choice of sorts. She could still turn back, she could
run out of the hotel, leave him and return to her room
and her mother, return to her cleaning job and all the
nagging at home, about getting away, finding a man,
she could go or she could give herself to him, this
stranger. She didn't know what to do. She did nothing.
She stood on the carpet waiting. She was cold. She
hadn't enough clothes on, didn't know, couldn't know
what effect this was having on him; she'd never been
with a man before. He put his arms round her.
Caressed her back and neck, her hair and her face, her
eyes; she stood looking at the bed, the big bed, as if
the bed was her way out, she wanted to get into the
bed, lose herself in it, pull the duvet round her and
sleep. I want to sleep with my clothes on, she said. She
lay down on the edge of the bed. He lay behind her,
behind her back with his uniform on. She could hear
his breathing, would he fall asleep? She closed her

eyes. Felt the way he pulled off her stockings and underwear. The way he pulled up her dress and moved his hands over her, slow, careful, hard. Was he crying? For a second she felt sorry for him, but then he pressed into her and held her firmly as if his hands had found something that belonged to him, he turned and moulded her as if she was some slight object, some slight, insubstantial object, she lost solidity, lost herself, body and hands and resistance, she lay with her face in the pillow. Buried her face in the pillow, as if she were ready to receive a punishment, she wanted to die. She was ready. Then she felt how he penetrated her, a short, hot pain; something burst within her, an opposition, a fear, she lost that as well now, she lost everything to that thrusting warmth, waves of warmth, a totally new heat. A totally new life. She sensed it in her body, a new gravity, a new age, then suddenly, a new fear: What had he done to her? Something inside her had awoken, she didn't need him. The oppressive air, the heavy body, she pushed him off, moved away from him and lay on the edge of the bed. She was burning inside, trembling with heat and agitation. He lay on the bed with his uniform on, his jacket open, his shirt open, his trousers, his mouth, he was asleep. She got up and opened the window. A new life. She didn't need him.

He fell in love with her; I think he fell in love with her, this young girl, Thea, who could have been his daughter. I'm certain he tried to stop seeing her. He went on seeing her, didn't want to see her, said that he wouldn't see her again; they met as if each time were the last, made love with the desperation of the first or last time, that's how it must have been, it couldn't have been otherwise: one day Thea came knocking at the door of the house where he lived. She was pregnant. His daughter opened the door, a young girl, Thea felt giddy, she almost fell, she wanted to fall on the doorstep and lie there: Is Espedal in? she asked. The daughter shook her head, made as if to shut the door. I've got to speak to him, she said, pleaded. Elly Alice closed the door and went in and woke her father: There's a girl at the door, she said. There's a girl at the door asking for Espedal.

Eivind, Eivind, Elly Alice shouted. She banged at the door, hammered at the door, no reply, not a sound, only the boy crying in the kitchen and Thea tugging at her hair, trying to haul her away from the door and out of the parlour. Why didn't he say anything? She wanted to lie down in front of the door and stay there. Let go of me, she said and Thea loosened her grip, let go of her hair and Elly Alice turned, went out into the kitchen and picked up the boy, carried him in her arms out of the kitchen and left the house. She pushed the boy along Inndalsveien at breakneck speed, down Bjørnsonsgate, he sat quite still in his pushchair, he'd stopped crying, sat in his pushchair looking at her with tear-filled eyes, frightened; suddenly she stopped the pushchair and bent down, flung her arms around the small boy, pulled him close to her as if he were older than he was, squeezed him to her and pressed her mouth to his cheek and held him tight while she whispered and forced her soft voice as hard as she could against his ear: I'm sorry, I'm sorry, she said over and over again: I'm sorry, darling Eivind. Elly Alice walked back to the house where she lived. It was Sunday. The third-floor window was open, she called out. She called out his name. After a minute she heard him on the stairs, she saw him behind the frosted glass of the street door, then he opened the door and let her in. Had he been asleep? He had been asleep, his face was tired, a heavy and impassive face,

he wasn't yet fully awake, he was distant and with-
drawn, he'd been asleep; it filled her with a sudden
fury, she wanted to tear at him and wake him, she
wanted to scream and wake him, he had to wake up
and be awake, she wanted to shout and spring at him,
but then she remembered the boy, he was standing
next to her clutching her coat; her head sank on her
chest and her knees gave way, she couldn't hold back
the tears, she tried, but they stuck there, in her legs
and stomach, in her breast and throat, in her mouth
and nose and eyes. There, there, he said. There, there.
He put one arm around her, lifted the boy with the
other and got them both up the stairs and into the
flat, it smelt of potatoes and meat, he'd cooked the
dinner. Now, let's eat, he said and took off her coat,
dried her eyes with the back of his hand, caressed her
hair and kissed her on the mouth, he smelt good, and
now she noticed: he had his Sunday best on, a freshly
ironed white shirt, black trousers and well polished
shoes, he'd dressed up.

He was a fine man, she didn't notice him.

She wept, she was ashamed of herself.

Always these tears. But now they were warm and
not cold, a warmth within her, she felt warmth for

him, embraced him and held him as she'd held the boy, did she feel sorry for him? He never complained, there was work, there was her and the child, and there was work again. When he wasn't at work, he moved restlessly about the flat mending things, he oiled the door hinges, put up a light, hung new curtains or wallpaper and laid lino on the kitchen floor. He made a cupboard, built a wall. He had a small workshop in the basement where he did some cobbling, scraped soles and repaired shoes, he made toys for his son. When he wasn't working, he occupied himself with lesser things, little jobs, trifles, he had to have something to do. She saw what work did to him, the way it distanced him from her, how it sapped his strength, took all his time, it wore him out. Work wore him out the way it had her father: he would soon be fifty and was already old, already exhausted, always tired. Two young children, he couldn't manage them. He couldn't manage Thea. When the working day was over, he sank into a lethargy of exhaustion, he couldn't be bothered with anything, and Thea had to do everything for him, she made dinner and supper, cleaned and tidied the house, attended to the children, got them to bed, she made breakfast and ironed his shirts, buttoned up the jacket of his uniform and sent him off to a place he didn't want to go to, he didn't want to go anywhere, he didn't want anything. He wanted to be alone, there was a yearning for loneliness in him. A desire for peace and quiet, for rest, perhaps he wanted to die; I think he had a death wish.

For a long time all I wanted was to go to bed early and stay there. But there was no time for that, there was so much that needed doing; the housekeeping had to be done, a teenager and her father; I made food and washed clothes, went shopping and worked about the house, cleaned and tidied, I helped her with her school work. The days were filled, the evenings too, and sometimes, more and more often, the nights; I sat at my writing table. I couldn't give up writing, it wouldn't be stopped, and it continued, against my will, to keep me working after I'd gone to bed: words and sentences chased through my brain as if my closed eyelids were the underside of a sheet of paper which someone was writing on, a dark sheet of paper on which the words stood out in full brilliance, they shone. These strings of words, of entire sentences, kept me awake. They shone out, like a lamp someone is turning on and off, they broke in and glowed as if they were full of meaning, of a deeper meaning, they contained an entire book. I had to write them down. I switched on my bedside light, wanting to write the words down, wanting to write them away, I made notes and wrote, but as soon as I'd turned off the light and closed my eyes, the words kept on coming, where from I don't know. I knew the sentences were connected with my work, that I needed them; I had to fix them on paper. I switched on the light again, got out of bed and went downstairs to my workroom, sat down at my writing table. Nothing. The sentences had gone, or they were unusable, meaningless, incomprehensible and without context; I couldn't use them. The time was four or five o'clock. For the second or third time I thought: It's time to go to bed.

This is the house at night.

Secluded, in a large garden, a narrow, white two-storey house, an attic window under the angle of the roof, the window is broken, bats fly in and out through a crack in the pane, he can hear them at night, even when he's asleep; they're in the house and they're in his dreams, not in a disquieting way but as a kind of reassurance, a protection. They hang from a cross-beam, their wings folded close to their bodies, heads down, eyes open, watching over the house. The house is tall with a steep slate roof, it resembles a tower. Almost uninhabitable, that's how it looks, on account of its wretchedness and dilapidation, an old house, draughty and cold, small rooms with lots of windows, they pepper the house, upstairs and down. The two floors are connected by a staircase. He hears her at night; she's coming home. First the front door, a gently rattling pane of glass, the door shutting, then the sound of feet on the stairs, quick, light, wary, it's the sound of coming home. He switches off the bedside light, closes his eyes, hears her undressing in the room next door. His elder daughter, going to bed. He feels it through the whole of his weary body, a trembling, warm or cold, as if water were streaming through him: a feeling of sheer happiness. She sleeps. He falls into her sleep, into the silence of the house. The house at night, he knows nothing of what goes on. The quick beat of wings. Rain against the window, the wind in the trees, someone standing in the room, he notices nothing of all this. What was it he dreamt? A thick, rough sheet of paper with organic letters, small protuberances on the paper, like congealed slime or pressed flowers, wheat or corn, but in black symbols, illegible and lovely, an unintelligible beauty, line after line, character after character: the unwritten book.

He dreamt of the unwritten book.

The book that would have everything in it.

The great, all-encompassing book; he dreamt about it, during the day as well, when he did the housework, when he washed the clothes and hung them up on the clothes line, when he was driving the car and when he sat at his writing table: he dreamt of the impossible book.

He did outlines and experiments, wrote a number of openings and drafts. He gathered them in his notebooks.

Notebooks: the dream of a book.

Henning wrote: I've failed with this poem. I fail. I fail at everything.

This, that, everything, it gets too much for me.

I give up. It's Sunday, Sunday the eighth of April; today my work ground to a halt, it's all falling to pieces: me, the book, everything.

It's Sunday the eighth of April. You get up. Splash cold water on your face, dress, in the same clothes, day after day. You work. April, September, day and night. You try to recreate an ordinary day, labour to describe a completely ordinary day, but can't. You give up. Change, put on a freshly laundered white shirt, clean trousers, your best shoes. You get ready to break down.

He gets up. He gets ready to break down.

He fails. He fails at everything.

His work, his family, his life, everything.

There, there, she says. There, there.

She puts her arm around him and kisses him on the mouth, he smells good and he's got dressed up, it's Sunday. He has spread a white tablecloth on the table, laid the Sunday plates and silver cutlery, the best glasses. Are we expecting visitors? she asks, he hushes her, hurries her, tells her to change, she's in front of the big wardrobe when she hears the knock at the door. It's Martin and Margit. Her sister and her boyfriend, Martin Øen. He's older than Margit, has a child from a previous marriage. Martin Øen is a bricklayer, he works as a bricklayer. He reminds Elly Alice of something she's read in a book: 'If he wasn't a good husband to his first wife, how can you possibly think he'll be a good husband to you?' He smells of aftershave lotion and alcohol, his white shirt is open all the way down to his stomach, he stands in the hall and lifts the boy, but the boy is scared and turns away, twists away and wants to get down on the floor again. He runs to his mother. Eivind, she says and buttons up her dress, goes out into the hall and embraces her sister. A surprise. Alfred's invited Martin and Margit to dinner. He's cooked the food, laid the table and tidied the flat while she was visiting her father in Inndalsveien. They sit down at the table. They eat. Roast pork with boiled potatoes and vegetables. Beer with the meal. Brandy with the pudding and coffee; the men smoke pipes, smoke and talk, the small dining room is filled with laughter and smoke, they open a window. Fresh spring air. Sharp, cold air and the low sun flashing on the windows on the other side of the harbour, the mountainside, the sunny side, its houses, its wooden villas; they eat and drink not thinking about the other side, about life there, they are content.

They are content, but Erling Johannessen is listless, restive, he has had a good dinner, two glasses of wine with his food, and now he wants to go out, go for a walk, for a stroll, the sun is shining, the evening sun is pouring through the living-room window, he'd like to go out but Aagoth asks him to stay in. She wants him to read to the two girls. She wants to bath them and put them to bed, and then she wants him to read to the two girls in bed, Else Marie and Unn, they like it when he reads, a fairy tale or two, and they fall asleep, or lie next to each other in the dark waiting for sleep to come. He would like to go out, the streets are still sunny, people strolling, up and down Torgallmenningen, out towards the marketplace, the Torget, or up the hill towards Vaskerelven and Vestre Torggate, up the steps towards the church of Johanneskirken and the park, he wants to go out for a walk, to look at the people, boys and girls, women and men, the young and unattached, it's spring, it's April, he's restless; he's still young. He is young and married. He is young and has two daughters. He is young and wants to go out, but Aagoth wants him to stay indoors. She wants him to read to the girls, just as he did yesterday and the day before; Sunday, Saturday, Friday, he's done what she wanted all weekend. Now he wants to go out, it's Sunday, his last day off before going back to work. He's got a good job, is well married, has a large flat in the centre of town; he isn't content. What does he want? He doesn't know, he wants to go out, he will go out; he puts on his hat and coat, defying for once all protests and accusations, he goes out.

My maternal grandfather, Erling Johannessen, went out. He crossed Torgallmenningen with his hat and stick, unshaven and with polished shoes, in a long, light-coloured coat, it was impossible to tell he was a father. I was frightened of him, in spite of the fact that he was always friendly and punctilious, always obliging and polite; I avoided him. I crossed Torgall-menningen pretending I didn't know him, crept past, cautious and shy. I was told, people often said he was the one I took after. It's not hard to imagine; me crossing Torgallmenningen dressed in a long, light-coloured coat, hat and dark glasses, stick and polished shoes, they don't know me.

I don't know myself. A cold, blue rain, which alters everything; the snow in the garden is washed off the trees and rinsed from the flowers, hard, the white disappears from the grass in front of the house in patches and strips, as when you tear the pages out of a book; I must flip back to autumn, November, September, the nineteenth or twenty-ninth, I write in my notebook: Tear these pages out.

A mask, my mask, it looks like my own face, that's the subtlety of it; I take the mask off and look like myself. I put the mask on and resemble the other, the one in disguise; he clothes himself in words.

Erling Johannessen goes out. He takes the lift down six floors, opens the lift gate, pushes open the front door and goes out into the streets, the city streets; he turns left for his normal route along the Allmenningen, past the Music Pavilion, walks along the right end of the Lille Lungegårdsvann lake, past the art galleries, towards the library, past the railway station and into the Terminus Hotel where he drinks a cup of coffee and leafs through the papers; his restlessness refuses to subside, walking doesn't help, he can't walk off the anxiety and decides to go home, he wants to get home before the girls have gone to bed, perhaps he'll be in time to read to them, he folds the paper and pays for the coffee. He would like to keep walking, he would like to leave everything behind, work, family, flat, everything, but the thought of such a complete change, such a departure, leaves him feeling exhausted and sad. He's happy he can walk home. He's been far away, in his thoughts he's been somewhere completely different, in a completely different life, now he's glad home isn't far away; he walks quickly and purposefully taking the shortest route through the city.

Torgallmenningen 7, sixth-floor flat, Sunday the eighth of April. Evening sun. It must be the most beautiful flat I've ever seen. Perhaps, for me, this absolute perfection in apartment form, is evoked and reinforced because my mother grew up here, it was her home. The flat was sold when my grandfather died, and in my eyes it was ruined, it was redecorated and modernized before being taken over by a new family, the flat was lost and so attained its permanence, inasmuch as I've always tried to recreate that flat everywhere I've lived and in the books I've written: might it be that I miss the flat more than I miss my grandparents?

You entered a long, narrow hall, it was practically a corridor where a row of closed doors gave you the

impression of a public building or an institution, the
doors were opened at fixed times and on fixed occa-
sions, there was the door to the bedroom, the dining
room, and, at the far end of the hall, the kitchen. At
the back of the kitchen there was yet another door,
which led into a small servant's room, a maid's room,
cramped under a gable roof, it wasn't hard to picture
someone being kept prisoner there. (A short girl with
long, dark hair and a white dress, we never saw her;
was there a secret door from this room to the walk-in
cupboard behind the desk in the living room? Was
there a flat within the flat, a secret within the family,
something that was hidden away? Yes, the unseen was
discernible here, they laboured under the weight of
things unspoken, an evil secret, and this made me fall
in love with the little girl who was locked up in the
maid's room.) My grandfather wrote diaries and letters, innumerable letters, his desk stood by a window
in the living room. Behind the desk was the cupboard
door, it was kept locked, as were the drawers of his
desk. This is a habit I've inherited, the habit and the
desk, it stands by the window as it should, the drawers are locked. On the desktop: a vase of flowers,
white chrysanthemums. Various pens, white paper, a

coffee cup. An ashtray, a knife, some books, photographs, a candlestick, and most beautiful of all, the table lamp. The writing lamp and the light from the window; life and written life, were these two different things? The living room was large and bright with windows all down the south-facing wall, a wall of windows, it looked out on to the patio where my grandmother grew flowers in pots and tubs, climbing roses on a trellis fixed to the high brick wall; it was a garden. A garden on the roof. Growing in towards the living room and continuing there, so it seemed, flowers were everywhere. Flowers and books, books in a long bookcase that had been specially made and took up the entire end wall, a wall of leather-bound books, red, black, brown backs with gilt and silver lettering, they ran across the wall like joined-up secret writing; I couldn't yet read, but the presence of this wall made me realize the importance of books. It was as if a stillness emanated from the books, from this part of the living room that resembled a library. A reading lamp, a chair. A radiogram, a radio and a gramophone in a large cabinet that stood next to the fireplace. A smoker's table. Several chairs, placed in a semicircle around the fireplace. In the middle of the living room was a circular occasional table which formed the focal point of the flat with the sofa and three chairs that went with it; no one ever sat in them, not while I was there, in any case it was difficult to imagine anything alive in the living room, it was dead, a space, a museum, life had been here once. The flat had everything, but it lacked love, there was no love between the husband and wife in this flat, rather a contempt which grew into hatred over the years, in the years after the two daughters had left home there was nothing but hatred remaining, hatred between man and woman, filling everything, every last room. It became obvious, the thing that had been obscured in the large flat, this contempt, this pent-up revulsion, it emerged and became thoroughly obvious; we saw and heard it now, the way they attacked and wounded one another, how they abused and humiliated each other, how they barked at each other, like two animals, him and her.

He arrives home, opens the front door, it's quiet in the flat; the two girls have gone to bed and Aagoth has fallen asleep between them, she's lying in the middle of the bed with the book open across her breast. The soft breathing, the beautiful face; he feels a stab at his heart, is it tenderness or bad conscience, a stab and he lingers in the doorway; I'd never be able to leave them.

He stands in the doorway looking at the three of them asleep on the bed. He would never be able to leave them. He goes into the living room, sits down at the desk, switches on the table lamp, it has turned dark outside, Sunday silent. He writes: Sunday the eighth of April. Then he lights a cigarette, pulls out a bottle from the locked cubby-hole in the desk, pours some into a glass. She's standing in the doorway. Tapping the door with one foot so that he'll know she's there, this irritates him, this knocking of the naked foot on the door.

You drink too much, Erling, she says.

I thought you were asleep, that you'd gone to bed, he says.

It's only half past eight, I read to the girls, they asked for you. I said you'd gone out, that you'd gone drinking, that you'd gone out for a drink, she lied. That's the truth isn't it?

He makes no reply. What should he answer; the truth, that doesn't interest him, he spends all his life and talents avoiding truths; he puts down the pen and looks at her, this small, dark figure, how is it that she takes up so much space, fills the flat and his life so completely, this thin face and dark, wavy hair. He did love her, didn't he?

Who are you writing to? she asks.

To my sister, Marie.

A letter to your sister, Marie, and what are you writing to your sister who lives just around the corner, just a few streets away, whom you see almost daily, and whom you speak to on the telephone, constantly, what have you got to tell your sister that she doesn't already know, what is it you're writing to your sister, Erling?

He doesn't answer this either. He can't be bothered to argue. Anything he says or does, she'll take amiss, distort, dispute; he's becoming taciturn, an increasing silence, it's a bigger and bigger part of him, this silence, it provokes her.

Are you telling her about us, about me, about how hard it all is, what are you telling her that you can't tell me? You're hiding, going away as often as you can, you're vanishing in front of our eyes, she says turning in the doorway. She goes out to the kitchen, perhaps she's going to use the bed in the small back room, the maid's room, sometimes she locks herself in. It's his punishment for not doing what she wants, what does she want? She goes and sleeps in the maid's room.

He remains at his desk. My mother inherited the letters he never sent and the diaries he wrote, they were in two boxes in the attic where we lived, and when she died the two boxes came to me, I took them at any rate, they belonged to no one and they lay in the loft like an unanswered message; I didn't read them, neither the letters nor the diaries.

He sits at his desk. She has left him, as she so often does, by locking herself in her own room. Then she'll pop up again next morning and next afternoon and evening only to leave him again, it's as if she wants, by continual desertion, to humiliate him without actually departing, she comes and goes, but always within the walls of the flat, as if he's living in a theatre, or an artificial home with a stage set and doors through which she exits and enters to deliver her lines and accusations. He doesn't like the theatre. He can't bear play-acting. But he can't take reality either, anything that's difficult and demanding, he can't take the truth, and this turns him into a prisoner, like a puppet that's got tangled up in its own strings, in its own inadequacy. He is chained to the flat and to his work. He is chained to his family and to her, Aagoth Constance Johannessen, he couldn't manage without her. That's the truth. And yet he sits at his desk writing about freedom; he could wish for a totally different life, in a totally different place.

Margit is sitting on Martin's lap, he's had too much to drink, he talks loudly and coarsely and does coarse things, the way he holds her, moves his hands over her clothes and under her clothes, she pushes his hands away, but they spring straight back as if they're attached by elastic or some mechanism that automatically draws his hand back to where she pulled them off: her thighs, breasts. That soft, naked skin; all week he's been working with bricks, hard, oblong stones that he lifts and lays and fills and fits together to make a wall, now his hands crave something different, something soft, and he's got a soft girl, a nice, curvaceous girl, he wants to touch her, feel her, all the time, why not, she pushes his hands away and they return like strong, heavy springs, his hands, resting on her thighs, her breasts. He forces his hands in under her blouse and clasps them tightly over her belly and hips, nice Margit, beautiful Margit, she hushes him and puts her mouth to his ear: We're in company, Martin, you must behave, Martin, I love you, Martin. Martin and Margit are visiting Alfred and Elly Alice, they're sitting in the dining room, on opposite sides of the table with its leftovers, beer bottles and cigarette ends, they talk and smoke, drink and discuss: trade-union matters. Wages. The future. It's Sunday the eighth of April. The future is bright. The future is open. The future is full of promise in Michael Krohnsgate. Elly Alice is in the bedroom checking that the boy is asleep, that he's breathing and lying in the right position, she tucks the duvet well around the sleeping body. The only child. Spoilt. The schoolchild. She harbours one overriding wish for her son: that he won't be like his father.

A mummy's boy. Cissy, he grew up in a tough street. They saw he was a mummy's boy, a lone child, he wasn't left alone, he wasn't left in peace. He had to teach himself to live in the street, find his place in the street, manage alone in the street, without brothers, without mates, he fought in the street, did well in the street, he was good at fighting. It was an ability he had, just as he was good at maths, or languages, he was good at giving and receiving blows. When he got home from school he had to hide the blood on his shirt and find an excuse for his split lip, the swollen eye, the ruined trousers. His mother washed his shirts, patched his trousers, cleaned and covered his cuts, she knew what he was going through, she saw it from the window.

She stood for whole days at the window and looked out at the street where she lived.

She stood for whole days at the window that looked out over the street where she'd remain all her life.

If she stood there long enough, she could see everything the street had been and would become: a narrow, mean street with long rows of brick houses on either side of the gravel road that led nowhere. She wanted to get away, she never would get away.

She stood at the window and saw him coming, alone, the lonely boy, back from school, in clothes that were too nice, polished shoes; he was pushed to the ground; today it was William, yesterday it had been Otto, tomorrow someone else; the boys stood in a circle around the two who were fighting, she didn't dare shout or run out into the street to help him, that would make everything worse, he'd have to look after himself. He did look after himself. He was surprised just how easily he could win fights, he was fiery and quick, he was good at fighting. But fighting in the street, the battle to find his place in the street and at school, was interrupted by a larger battle: the great and all-encompassing war, it cut him short, disturbed him; he was taken out of school, sent away from the street, away from his mother, he was moved out to relatives in the country.

He wanted to stay at home. The war didn't scare him but the thought of being parted from his mother was awful, it frightened him.

He wasn't frightened, what was there to be frightened of, in the street, at home, he wasn't frightened, he was frightened of losing his mother.

I'll visit later, she said, in the summer.

The summer. How long was he going away for?

A few days, a week, perhaps two, but not more, never in a million years; he couldn't manage without her.

One day, it was a Friday, his father came to fetch him from school. His father stood outside the school gates with a pack on his back and a large bag in his hand: We're off now. But the boy didn't want to go anywhere, not alone or with this father he barely knew, he wanted to go home. He wanted to run, scared by the father who stood waiting: We're off now. We're off, but the boy only wanted to run away, he walked unwillingly across Danmarksplass and through the park. They crossed the city centre and walked towards the quay from where the boat sailed in the evening, in the darkness of evening, a boat without lights, they travelled in the dark.

They lay next to each other in the cabin, father and son, they'd never been alone together before, they travelled like two strangers. His father was silent and uncommunicative. He rarely spoke to the boy. You're going to your relations in Sunnfjord, he said. Your mother's family, a farm in Espedal, they're kind people, he said, and your mother will visit in the summer. It's not safe for you at school or in the street. It's the Germans, he said. We're at war with the Germans, they've taken over the shipyard. They've taken over Michael Krohnsgate and Laksevåg and all the rest of

Bergen and the country, he said. Do you understand what I'm saying? The boy nodded. He knew. It was war, and he wanted to be with his mother.

He lay in the cabin next to his sleeping father; his breathing and the engines pulsed in the darkness like some hostile heart; he lay in the bowels of the boat that was taking him the wrong way, to a place he'd never been and to people he didn't know, he wanted to go the opposite way, as fast as possible, back to the house, to the street, to school, to the mother who needed him, he needed her. It was war. Why were they sending him away from the war at home to a war in a place he didn't know; he would lose the war, he would lose everything. Light came with the morning, a hard, white light that sliced down between the mountains and into the shining fjord, as if they were sailing on ice, as if the passenger boat glided along in a tunnel of light; it hurt his eyes, all that whiteness, all that new-ness, the snow-capped peaks and steep ravines down to forested hillsides and green pastures that ran out to the sea. He noticed the farms that lay hemmed in by the water's edge, linked only by paths and narrow gravel roads; he was a captive. He sat by the window in the boat and ate some of the food his father had brought along in the pack: clothes and shoes, school-books and writing paper, shirts and underwear, all had been carefully folded and placed in the pack by his mother, he wanted to hoist it on his back and walk home. It was only a matter of time, a week, a month, and he'd walk home, on foot across the mountains, back to the city, to the street, to school, to his mother; he pictured it in his mind's eye: how he'd leave his room and the isolated farm, early in the morning, be-fore anyone stirred, he'd set off with the pack on his back. The passenger boat was sailing into Sognefjord and the boy was already on his way back, home. He was travelling in the opposite direction, he was going his own way.

In May the last patches of snow vanished from the meadow, and the snow melted in the mountains, it ran down the mountainsides in rills and small waterfalls that splashed over rocks and soil, a tumult of water in the forest where earth and old roots, twigs and stones were torn from the ground and carried down in a strong, brown current towards the river which burst its banks and lay almost static in great pools in the meadow for days, nights, until the river girded up its loins and pushed all the water in great heaves and white torrents out into the fjord. The sun shone. The earth steamed. A thin, white mist above the trees, windflowers on the ground and the streams quietened. Birdsong. The first garden birds, wagtail and blackbird, great tit and sparrow. The black shadow of larger birds, raven or hawk, eagle or owl, a bird of prey. Deer tracks on the edge of the forest. A glimpse of hare, of fox. It was a strange world to the boy. The ewes lambed. A foal lay in the grass, there were chickens in the hen coop. The cows calved, potatoes were planted, carrots and turnips sown. Swedes and radishes. The apple trees blossomed, white flowers like snow in the trees, plums and apples. It was a new world to the boy: natural things and the work of the farm. He rose early and helped the farmer in the cowshed. He followed his mother's uncle to work, walked behind the farmer in the meadow, up and down behind horse and plough, they worked, boy and man. Mended tools, split wood. Stacked birch logs, fed the stove, fetched eggs from the hen coop and drove lambs and ewes out of the barn, out into the meadow, it was work, it was a game. In the mornings he sat in his room studying his schoolbooks. He read a book by Mark Twain. He cut an aspen withy, attached a string and hook to it, and went for long trips along the river, dug for worms and fished the pools, early and late, he enjoyed fishing. He liked walking in the mountains, went up through the gate at the back of the house and followed the forest road until he reached the path to the summer farms. He lay on his back in the grass letting the sun warm his body until his skin burnt and prickled. Alone. He liked being alone; I know that he likes being alone, he sits in his room reading the newspapers, looking out of the window and smoking cigarettes, not answering the phone or opening the door, sits pent up like this for days without showing any sign of life, he got it from his father and it's been passed on to his son, it must be a family trait. He lay in the grass feeling the warmth from the sun. A stream ran past the summer farms and he drank the cold, clear water before pressing on towards the highest summit where he halted and looked out across the valley. Did he want to go home? He didn't know, his mother would be coming in a month, a month until midsummer, he missed her but not so much as before. He didn't miss school or the street, his friends or his classmates. His mother wrote to say that the school had been bombed, many had died and their house in Michael Krohnsgate had no windowpanes: We can't close the doors in the flat because the whole house is askew after the bombing. He wrote back to say that he'd seen German soldiers, they came to the farm to get butter and eggs, milk and potatoes, they were polite and paid for their purchases. His mother wrote that she couldn't come in the summer after all, she had to stay with his father, help his father as best she could, he needed her and it wouldn't be long before the war was over, she was certain of it, the war will soon be over, and you'll soon be home. He sat in his room reading the letter, looking out of the window and not answering when they called him from the living room, didn't open when they knocked at his door, he wanted to be alone. He missed her and he didn't want to go home.

The family was having dinner in the best room, the table was spread with a white cloth and china plates, silver cutlery and candlesticks, they were celebrating the boy's birthday. A small party, there was Jakob the farmer and Astrid his wife and their two sons, Aksel and Hjalmar who'd come home to help with the haymaking. There were the little girls, Mathilde and Irene, they sat next to the boy on the bench; he'd turned thirteen that August.

In September the trees turned colour from green to yellow and red, a fire in the treetops, it flared up along the mountainsides and in the forest; he felt it in his body, he was in love. There was a remnant of summer in the gusts of wind, a cold prick of winter; the boy worked hard, harder than necessary, he was frightened of being sent home.

Jakob and his sons mowed the second crop of hay with scythes, they raked the newly cut grass into piles and threw it into the wagon where the boy stood wearing outsized boots tramping the grass down before the horse hauled the load up the hill to the cowshed: we dug our hayforks into the grass and spread it out where the walls of the barn were slatted and the wind could dry it.

In the middle of the month Mathilde and Eivind picked apples on the farm, he climbed the trees and put the apples carefully in the basket which he let down on a rope to Mathilde who sorted them and laid them out in boxes which he lugged into the cellar: then we gathered the plums in the same way, and when we'd finished with the fruit trees, we started on the bushes, we picked blackcurrants and gooseberries, raspberries and redcurrants.

Astrid boiled up the berries and made jam which was put in jars and juice which was poured into bottles, they stood ranged in shining rows on shelves in the cellar, jar upon jar with labels that glowed in the dark; with a knife each, Mathilde and Eivind sat among animal carcasses and dried fish, cleaning rhubarb and dicing it so that it could be boiled as soup or stewed fruit: we picked bilberries and whortleberries, cloudberries and mushrooms, picked everything edible and went into the forest for as long as we could, as often as we could, until it was dark.

They walked in the forest as often as they could, following animal tracks and hearing guns, hare and deer were being shot, grouse were being shot; the birds hung in the cellar tied together with wire, their small heads lolled with closed eyes next to wings and feathers, the feathers had begun to turn white. Snow fell in the mountains. Frost and ice hardened the forest floor. The marshes froze and they could slide on the smallest mountain tarns, the meadow was snowy and white. There was little to do on the farm. Mathilde went to school, Eivind sat by the stove in the living room and waited. Sometimes he read. He waited for her to come back from school. Occasionally he wrote letters to his mother, shorter and shorter letters, less frequent letters, the last written in November, and that same month he was sent home, against his will, and before the war was over; they said he must be home for Christmas, but it wasn't necessary, it was far too soon, he didn't want to go home. He regretted writing those letters to his mother; they'd been written to re-assure her, but they'd made her anxious. The letters had had the opposite effect of what was intended; he was enjoying himself and that made her unhappy. It was probably because he was managing without her. It was probably because he'd mentioned Mathilde. He had to learn to lie. He had to learn to guard secrets. He had to learn about the things that touch on love.

Now it happened, the terrible thing, the accident which augured that our house was no longer sacred. Was it what I'd been waiting for, this terrible event, or was it simply an incident that meant nothing beyond what happened, a natural occurrence, although right in my garden, and it certainly was terrible. I was sitting

working at my desk as usual. Amalie had gone to
school, we'd had breakfast together as we always did,
she ran for the schoolbus, always at the last moment,
she sprinted down the gravel path and disappeared
through the gate with her schoolbag slapping against
her back, she never missed the bus. I went with her to
the door, stood on the step and watched her run off.
The cat came from its sleeping place. I gave it some
food and sat down at my desk. At eleven-thirty the
post came. When Agnete died, I took on the house
and both her daughters; I took on the cat; I took on
everything: her family, her men, her problems, her
past, everything. I moved into the house, anything else
was unthinkable, the girls must continue their lives in
familiar surroundings. Three times a day I fed the cat.
It lived its own untrammelled life in its haunts, in the
garden, under the drying porch and around the house,
the cat slept and lived outside but was almost always
within view; I saw it from where I was sitting at my
desk. The cat lay in its usual places in the sun, it had
its habits and fixed routines, just like me. We kept
close to the house, we took our walks, mine was usually in the direction of the shop, past the farm with
the farmer's untethered dogs, they rushed towards me,

every day, four black dogs, agitated and aggressive, they only left me alone when the farmer whistled. I'd been for my walk, now I was sitting at my desk looking out of the window as usual. The cat lay under the apple tree, where there was a small depression in the grass, perhaps the cat could feel the warmth from the tree's roots; I often wondered why it lay just there, the cat curled up and almost disappeared in the hollow beneath the tree. Just then I heard something like the onset of a storm. The sudden wind and storm of something surging around the house, I heard feet, running feet, a wind of feet, they were out of control, they were caught up in an instinct of chase and attack. The next moment I saw the dogs like two black projectiles round the side of the house, they came from the back of the house and shot round the corner, straight at the cat which was lying under the tree in the garden. It was two of the farmer's dogs, my heart seemed to stop, heart and time stopped, and what happened next happened quickly and slowly at the same time; the cat sprang up and tried to run, it was too late, it was caught in its dash, the first dog grabbed one hind leg with its mouth and yanked the cat to the ground while at the same moment the other dog hurled itself on to the prey and sunk its jaws into the cat's neck; the two dogs tugged in different directions, pulled and tore the cat between them, it screeched or hissed or whatever that noise was, a dreadful sound, a frightful scream, and I jumped up from my seat and ran out into the garden. For a moment I hoped the cat was dead. For a moment I hoped it was the end of the cat, and the end of the house, the end of Askøy and life on the island; I'd had enough. But the cat was alive and the dogs dropped their prey when I came running out into the garden; they dropped the cat at my feet and stood there looking at me, as if they were waiting for some reward. They had obeyed their instincts, completed the hunt, and now they wanted their reward; I kicked the nearest dog in the muzzle. It whined and sank, crept backwards towards the other dog which barked. Would they attack? I looked about for a stick or a stone or anything I could beat the dogs with. I wanted to break every bone in their bodies. I wanted to smash their skulls, and carry the two carcases down to the farmer. I would drop them outside his door, and I'd use the stick on the farmer and do to him what I'd done to his dogs, but I found no stick, and the dogs ran off; I was left alone with the cat. What should I do? It was lying in the grass. It was in shock; I saw how its eyes were distended and wide open, as if they were opening completely before its eyes burst and the cat died. But it didn't die. The cat tried to creep and drag itself away, as if it knew what I stood there thinking; I'd have to kill it.

I had to kill the cat. The dogs had attacked and almost torn it to pieces, but they hadn't killed it. They'd left that to me. I'd looked after the cat ever since Agnete became ill and I moved into the house; each time I saw the cat, I thought of her: she lay here in the grass, dying.

She lay here in the grass, dying. Didn't she say she'd been torn to pieces, that she'd been torn apart by her parents, by her men, that life ripped and tore at her so much that she fell apart? Didn't she say that we were the ones who'd destroyed her, we who were closest to her, we made it all the more difficult for her, she said, not easier, we made it all the more difficult and finally totally impossible for her? We who were closest to her, her parents and her men, hadn't helped her, hadn't made things easier for her, we'd pulled and torn her to pieces, like dogs, she said. Each time I saw the cat, I thought of her; I thought of the cat as a remnant of her, sometimes I even thought of the cat as her, it stood in the doorway and I called to it using her name. Yes, I did. I used her name to the cat. I told the cat that things would work out, that we'd manage, her two daughters and me. The cat stood in the doorway and looked at me. I told the cat that it was difficult living alone with two girls. It's a difficult house, I said, draughty and cold, hardly more than a cabin, a cabin in the forest, far from the town, on an island, just the way you wanted. I said that I often felt like giving up, that I needed help, but that your nearest and dearest, your parents and your men, made everything more difficult for me. Your parents and your men are making everything impossible for me, I told the cat. Sometimes I'd get furious, furious with the cat, and chase it away, blame it for all my woes, for my whole situation; I didn't treat it kindly. Perhaps it was my fault that the cat finally gave up, that in the end it died, that it got torn to pieces by the dogs. They didn't kill it; I had to put the cat out of its misery, and the day after I killed it and buried the body behind the drying porch in the garden, I made up my mind to move.

Where would we live? We had nowhere to move to; I hadn't much money, only enough to get by. I tried to conceal it as well as I could, from the neighbours and my daughter, but we were close to poverty, perhaps we were poor. I wrote to earn money. The truth was that I'd never written as well anywhere as I did at the house on Askøy. Money was a necessity, and I divided up the day into working periods, the week into working days: I thought of writing as necessary work. I had fixed routines. I had a workroom. I worked. Like my father before me, and his father before him, we worked. We worked to keep poverty at bay, this familial weakness, this constant worry about not having enough money, about not being able to support a family, it was inherited, we were and remained a family of workers, we worked to earn money, and I wrote as if I had a job in a factory.

This is what the day looks like:

White.

Crocus. Lilies. Snowdrops. Cigarettes.
Sun. Something black.

Even early in the morning, in all that strong light;
something or the other black. It doesn't disappear.

Something bad. Something dark. It becomes visible
and then turns invisible again.   White.

Something or the other black.   During the day.

And the same at night, something white.
Something or the other terribly white during the night.
And the same during the day, something black.

It's nameless and afterwards it gets its name back.

The names come. A thin, white mist. Gradually a hint
of blue. A cold stirring in the air and this silvery blue
colour that forms on the windowpane. Ice flowers. Sun.
First a light, pale yellow shaft, and later the way the light
expands on the glass like a gas flame, orange, hot: how
all the objects in the room have their clear shapes
restored, how the bed becomes a bed. How the trees
become trees, the flowers flowers, the faces vanish
and the house becomes a house. The rooms become
inhabitable, recognizable, how the names return.

Everything that doesn't materialize, is painful.

Everything that doesn't materialize. Doesn't go away.

You shouldn't be alone too long. You shouldn't lie like
this in the darkness, arms wrapped around yourself.
Morning is coming. The names return and the day
begins. The day begins with the first sentence: You
shouldn't be alone too long, ageless, nameless.

The colours come. You're dazzled by all the white in the yellow, the white in the grey, the white in the flowers and in the trees, the black between the branches and the leaves that shoot, first as hard, green buds; they open out, a fan of leaves, and in the midst of this very blossoming, something black.

Something hard. Almost invisible, practically mute and colourless, and yet a focus, something in the midst of the flower, in the midst of the day which the day contains and covers like a petal or the light above the darkness in leaf-like shapes before the middle opens and becomes a beginning.

In the midst of the beginning, something black. And the same in the essence of finality that is hard, something unchanged and black.

I can still hear her name, even though her name has gone. Those first sounds, the insanity of the birds, take shape in a dream, a bright, gauzy and static dream, like an image, or a face, or a cobweb; and in the midst of the dream, something black.

The black in the eyes, or in the fly, in the fly's back and the thin, dark nick between head and body, the transparent wings and the tracery in the wings of flies that get caught in the spider's web; a buzzing sound that gets louder and sharper, metallic, machine-like, before it goes completely quiet.

And the drilling machine, the drill, the machine that's pressed hard against the rock face, makes a crack in the stone that opens up in a black fissure, a deep wound in the rock that breaks and divides in two; the rock is crushed and broken into smaller and smaller fragments, they lie strewn over the grass like parts of a larger body, pieces of flesh and entrails, heart, lungs and throat, a head and flies buzzing over the warm animal or human remains, something that has lain in the ground, and the drilling machine that's pressed hard against the surface, is raised and pounds the thin air, is turned off, it is stopped and goes quiet in the same instant as the fly.

A building site, on the slope to the north of the house, a stone's throw from the house, on the seaward side, they're building a playschool. The sound of the work, it arouses the desire to work. The desire to destroy. The sound of children.

youwaitforityouwaitforitasforan accidentora punishmentyouliethereinbedwaiti ngf ortheawful soundofchildrenyoucan'tbearitthe soundofpastand futureinthesamecry.

Children, you can't bear them.

One must maintain certain systems. One needs children, they're necessary.

A certain activity. It will, it must continue, it's necessary. The sound of necessity, I can't stand it. It's seven o'clock. It's morning. I already know what the day will look like: you send your child away. You entrust your child to the manufacture of childhood. It's necessary.

I hear her waking up in the room next door, the children's room, two beds, no children; she's already older than her age, her younger sister has moved out. Everything's changed, the room is the same, the same white walls, pictures of horses, a school desk and lamp, some new clothes, some new smells, a few cosmetics, they lie hidden at the foot of the bed, beneath some books, a small mirror, the face mirror; a new face, a mask, naturally, the teenager's mask, it says: Everything's normal, everything's fine; but nothing is normal, and perhaps things aren't fine; but the mask is soothing, it's reassuring in all its disquieting garishness.

A new age, a new body, but the room is unchanged, the room is the same, it's caught up in something that has been, something that ought to have changed, but remains, seems to hang in the air, only connected to the rest of the house by thin threads, it's caught up in something that's been lost.

She wakes. The day begins. I'm happy as I don't have to go anywhere.

When she goes out of the door, on her way to school, I sit there waiting for her to come home. I wait for her to come home: one day she'll phone and say that she's spending the night at a girlfriend's, one day she'll phone and say she'll sleep over at a friend's, one day she'll phone and say she's moving to the city, that she's moving to another town; I'm waiting for it.

I'm waiting to be deserted. One day the phone will ring and she'll say she's moving to another country, possibly we won't be seeing each other that often, seldom, presumably, more and more seldom, probably, she doesn't know when it will be, perhaps at Christmas, perhaps the New Year, perhaps not at all. In the summer, she'll say.

I'm waiting for summer.

I'm waiting for her, why hasn't she come, school ends at half past two, it's now nearly four, dinner is ready, why hasn't she come? One day she won't come. But today she arrives, late, she's been talking to Oskar, standing at the turning place for almost an hour and talking to Oskar, what were they talking about?

What do they think about, what do they do? Give it two or three years, and I'll be left with nothing.

I'm waiting to be on my own.

The morning sun warms the timbers of the house. The white house. The white bed. I'm waiting for the first sentence: 'Then the light suddenly pours in and hides us completely.'

She vanishes in all this whiteness. 'Like Mum who isn't there even when she seems to be.' A transparent absence. Something white in all the whiteness. Something painful. Something painful that conceals itself within the visible. It doesn't disappear.

Something that's white in the strong morning light. It becomes visible and then turns invisible once more.

Something that's terribly white during the day. And at night.

A white mother. So transparent that it's painful.

She doesn't disappear.
Ever
Not
while what doesn't exist causes pain.
She causes pain
the good mother
who doesn't exist
who didn't exist
when she was here.

This is what the day looks like:

White.

Rhododendron. Hawthorn. Lilacs. Cigarettes.
Sun. Something black.

A repeat of yesterday and of tomorrow. Something
or the other black during the day. And the same tomorrow, something black.

It doesn't disappear.

I wake and discover a strange arm right by my head,
an old arm, its skin puckered and loose, loosened
from the muscles and the arm itself, like something
superfluous, something that doesn't belong to the arm
so much as it does to time; something yet to come,
whose arm is it? I lie there, half awake, and study the
arm, it's yellowish with small brown flecks and some
thin, dark fissures or lines, they run across the arm as
if, during the night, someone has cut the skin with a
razor-sharp scalpel, imperceptible, almost, faint lines
on which are written, as I now see, a single word.

It could have been my granny's arm. It could have been my mother's arm, but in that case I must have lain in my mother's arms as an adult, and that never happened, never could have happened, and yet I recognize my mother's arm.

So it could be my arm, or my mother's arm in mine, it must have grown there during the night.

Or, I must have assumed her gestures. I place my hand against my cheek just as she used to place her hand against her cheek or as she could have placed her hand against my cheek.

Or is it a stranger's arm: I'm lying next to an elderly woman.

In the folds of skin along the arm I can read the word elderly.

A loving arm? The way you hug yourself in the night.

My arm. It belongs to my mother.

My mother was a secretary. She spent most of her adult life sitting in front of a typewriter.

I inherited my first typewriter from her.

After only a few years I had her hands, now I have my mother's arm, it has grown up in my own.

I write with her hands, her movements; we do the same work, we produce sentences and words.

We sit in front of the typewriter, hour after hour, day after day, year in year out, we have the same slightly rounded shape that crouches over the machine, head seeming to hang in thin air between the shoulders, a back that refuses to turn round, that won't allow itself to be distracted and remains rigid in the same firm, proud position, we sit with our backs to the door.

We work. In my own way I keep her alive; I sit like her, tap the keys of the keyboard, hammer the black letters on to the white paper, fill page after page with sentences and words. Then I light a cigarette. I hold the cigarette in my left hand, between index finger and middle finger gripping it just above the filter, raise my head and prepare my mouth to receive the white roll that's turning black at the far end, a black edge or ring that burns down the paper with each puff, with each inhalation, we breathe the blackness in. In my own way I've taken over her death; we smoke in the same way, write in the same way, make notes with our right hand and keep the cigarette in our mouth as we transfer the notes to the white sheet with both hands on the electric machine.

I wake up and discover that my arm has got older, it's lying next to my head; during the night I've placed my hand against my cheek and it makes me think of my mother, I can see her so clearly, she's lying next to me in the way she never did: she's lying next to me and laying her hand on my cheek and I miss her dreadfully.

The names come. The colours come. The sounds, the smells; the day begins and finds its way back to what was yesterday and will be tomorrow: a perfectly ordinary day. A good day. A working day. The perfect day; the day that resembles other days, that doesn't stand out, that fits into the run of ordinary days. I'm not going anywhere. I'll sit at my typewriter. Thursday, twelfth April; today I'll write about my mother.

Eivind Espedal Olsen moved back to Michael Krohnsgate after spending the final few months of the war with relations in Sandefjord, on a farm at Fjaler; he'd got taller and stronger, a dark, lanky boy who moved back home, and whose only desire was to move out. Away from the cramped flat, away from the street, the long, grey working class street with its brick houses in rows on each side of the road; he didn't want to go on living there.

More and more frequently, after school hours, he'd walk into the city, across Danmarksplass and through the park, past the Johanneskirken church and down the steps to the city centre. He'd walk the streets. Walk up and down the city streets and look at the shop windows, stand outside the hotels and tearooms and gaze at the girls. He liked wandering around the city. He'd cross the Torget and watch the boys selling fish, they were his own age, they were working. He wanted to work. He wanted to get away. Twice a week he went for boxing training. He trained at the Bjørgvin Boxing Club which occupied a gym in the middle of town. The changing room had steel lockers and a row of benches, he had his own locker. Some of the lockers contained pictures of famous boxers, others of nude girls. He dressed. Socks, shorts, vest. He wound stretchy bandage round his hands, tightened his shoelaces, put his gum shield and gloves in a cloth bag which he took with him into the gymnasium. He skipped. He did push-ups, sit-ups, warmed up. Joined the other boxers in a line moving forwards and backwards, feinted and punched, ducked and jabbed. He shadow-boxed. Pounded the punchbags. Hit the trainer's open gloves, they sparred in pairs, changed partners, had bouts in the overcrowded place. Twice a week. At the weekends there were competitions, at home and away, he boxed against opponents from Stavanger and Trondheim, from Oslo and smaller places. He boxed against Russians and Finns, Swedes and Germans, Englishmen, boys from streets that were like our streets, families that resembled our families, workers' families, workers' sons, they fought other working-class boys. Outside the training venue, in the street, stood the girls, the girls who'd watched the training bouts from their places on the window ledges; they stood outside the hall and waited for the boxers to come out. Some of the boys walked past, some of the boys halted, the bravest stopped and exchanged a few words, chatted. Flirted. Eivind had noticed one of the girls, she wasn't dressed like the others, didn't behave like the other girls, she seemed reserved and out of place, he thought she had a difficult look. She always had expensive clothes, a particular style; her short hairdo and the way she spoke, a special inflection, condescending, as if she were too good to be where she was, outside the training venue, why was she standing here? Why was she standing with girls who weren't like her, she stuck out. Perhaps she came from a better family, a superior family, why was she standing outside the hall waiting for the boxers? One evening she would tell him that she was there because her parents didn't allow her to wait outside the gym. She wasn't allowed to be with the girls she was with. There were lots of things she wasn't allowed; I smoke because I'm not allowed to, and I'm standing here because the girls my parents want me to be with, bore me. I do as much as I can of what I'm not allowed, I certainly wouldn't be allowed to stand here talking to you, she said. They walked away from the gym together, towards the city centre. So are you walking with me, because you're not allowed to? he asked. I don't know why I'm walking with you, do you want to see where I live? she asked. I always get home half an hour later than I'm told to. This is the door, it's locked, I haven't got the key, I'm not allowed the key to the door where I live. My mother always says that she won't be like her mother, but she's become exactly the way she says she shouldn't be. She's become just as strict as she says her mother was, maybe even stricter, she said and rolled her eyes. She's become like her mother. BUT I'LL NEVER BE LIKE MY MOTHER, she said. I won't make the same mistakes as her and her mother before her, and all the other mothers, she said. I'll never treat my daughter, or son, the way she treats me, and that's for sure, she said. He nodded. He shrugged his shoulders. They stood outside the entrance to Torgallmenningen 7. She lived right in the heart of the city, above it, on the sixth floor. He read the names on the door plate, her name was Johannessen. She pushed the bell. Aagoth and Erling Johannessen it said on the plate. My mother will be coming down, you'd better go now, she said.

I'll never be like my mother, she used to say to me, continually; I'll never treat you the way my mother treated me, I've made my mind up on that, she said. She was the strictest and most difficult person I've ever known; she turned into exactly what she said she never would. She became like her own mother, maybe worse, I don't know, it's difficult to weigh up love and stringency. I'm often told I'm like my mother. People often say, it's frequently remarked that I've become like her; it's extraordinary how similar we are, in looks and in temperament, they say. My father says: You're just like your mother. Just as headstrong and difficult, just as unpredictable and excitable, you flare up at the slightest thing and can't bear criticism, just like your mother, she couldn't bear to be told off, just like you. You've become just like your mother, he says and turns away, he turned and crossed Torgallmenningen,

glanced up at the roof of the building and the flat on
the sixth floor; she thinks she's quite somebody, he
thought as he walked across Ole Bulls Plass, past the
Hotel Norge, across Festplassen towards the railway
station and Danmarksplass. Will she do what she's not
allowed, will she be standing outside the gym as usual?

She wasn't there. Not on Tuesday or on Thursday, he
looked for her, but didn't dare ask her friends where
she was or why she wasn't there, perhaps they didn't
even care. Maybe they were relieved she was absent?
Was he relieved she wasn't standing there? The following week she was there again, standing in the midst
of the girls, smoking. Wearing a black jumper and
a long, black skirt. Her hair short, black. She was
entirely black, as if she wanted to hide in the twilight.
As if she wanted to hide from him, but she stood out,
he went to where she stood smoking; I've been under
a week's house arrest, she said. They walked through
the city together. This time I mustn't be late, I've told
them about you and that you walked me to the door.
Who is he, what's his name, where does he live, what
are his parents called, what sort of work do they do?
My mother wanted to have the lot, but I didn't know

a thing. And then I was put under house arrest and told I wasn't to see you again. He couldn't raise his eyes, stared at his shoes. So is that why you're walking with me now? he asked. But this made her angry, suddenly she flared up and screamed at him and called him names and pummelled him. Her fists and her fit of rage amused him and he wrapped his arms around her, he did it automatically, as in a fight, he wrapped his arms around her and held her tight. I'm called Eivind, he said. Eivind Espedal Olsen. My father works at the shipyard, my mother has a part-time job in a florist's, we live in Michael Krohnsgate, he said. She calmed down at this, lowered her arms and went quiet. Then she began to cry. She shook and gasped for breath, for a second he thought she was about to fall, that she'd fall down in the street, he put his arm around her and held her up. Please let go, she said. He let go. She stood on the pavement crying. I'm doomed, she said. He'd never heard anyone talk like that before. I'm doomed, she said again. Whatever I do, it always goes wrong, it's bound to, she said.

She didn't want to meet him any more. And yet she was there as usual outside the gym. He was the handsomest of the boxers, tall and dark, with a black lock that hung down over his pale face. A narrow, refined face that was marred by the thick eyebrows and all the cuts he had above his eyes, his split lips, sometimes his eye was puffy, there was blood on his collar, sticking plaster on his face, she couldn't show him off to anyone, she couldn't present him to her parents. Those big hands, the jacket with arms too short and the trousers that ended too far up his legs, the strange shoes he wore, they could have been his father's. He came out of the gym and she turned away. She'd expected him to come over to her, or call her name, she'd expected him, if he'd had to, to shout her name or grab her by the arm and drag her off with him, but she heard nothing and nothing happened. When she turned back to look at him, he wasn't there. He'd walked past. She felt it like a slap in the face. How dare he? Who did he think he was? He walked past. She saw his back and his neck, the way he took long, quick strides down the street and round the corner, she felt it like a stab in the breast. Just as he disappeared round the corner, it was as if the breath was sucked out of her, it amazed her; the slap, the stab, the breath, she couldn't understand why she was reacting like this. She saw his back and neck and knew in that instant that she would never, ever, allow him to walk past her, to ditch her in that way. He wasn't her type. She wasn't even certain whether she liked him, but when she saw his back and the way he walked, part of her wanted to run after him, wouldn't let him go. She wouldn't let him go. At night, when she lay in the bedroom, next to her sister in bed, he was the one lying by her side; he lay with his back towards her and she lay behind him and looked at the beautiful, narrow neck, the neck continued into the body and out into the shoulders, the transition between the short, dark hair and the pale skin, the ears and the back of his head, she lay behind him stroking his back with her hand. When he turned towards her, she saw only the sticking plasters on his face and the swollen eyes, the cuts on his mouth, and she lost him, was unable to conjure him up, was unable to see herself with him. When she looked into his face, she saw nothing but problems, she imagined her father, she heard her father's voice: It's impossible, Else. Yes, it's impossible, she said.

She was in love; I believe she was in love, she must have fallen in love with him. Perhaps she was attracted by the way he avoided her and made it obvious that he could manage well enough in his own world, without her.

His world, maybe it was better than hers?

Her world was a sham, and she was imprisoned in it. She was locked up in a large flat and guarded by two parents who said they were concerned for her own welfare, but she didn't want to be like them. His world seemed freer, more dangerous, stronger, his world frightened her.

Perhaps she was drawn by his appearance, his good looks, he was handsomer than anyone else she'd seen; all those boys with good surnames, surnames that meant so much to her mother, and which she never stopped talking about, this one and that one, this family and that, they were her mother's names, her mother's ambitions, not hers, she didn't like them. She wanted to defy her parents. She didn't want to let them decide whom she met and whom she went with. She didn't want to be like them. They didn't love each other. They lived together like two shadows, each in their corner of the flat; they shouted at each other or wouldn't speak for days. They slunk past each other,

locking themselves in their rooms. There was a perni-
cious silence between them. A dreadful hush in the
flat where they lived, where they were imprisoned. She
was sixteen and had to get out, out of the silence, out
of the pretence, that secure pretence; she had to defy
herself, do something she didn't want to do, she would
throw herself into an impossible relationship.

It could have been like that, it must have been like
that; I like to sit here at my writing table and think
about the first time she invited him home. It must
have been the first time she'd ever done something
impossible, something that could never work out,
it wouldn't be the last time. There are photographs of
the event; my grandfather was an amateur photogra-
pher and he photographed the various scenes as if he
wished to document a theatrical production: the lav-
ish dinner table in the dining room, the coffee service
and cakes on the occasional table in the living room,
the white curtains, the crystal vases of flowers, the
candlesticks, the damask tablecloth with silver dishes
and napkins, the glasses of lemonade, the young,
besuited boy raising his glass in a toast, the young girl,
dressed in black who's looking down, who looks down

each time her father tries to photograph her. The mother who has dressed up, who has laid the tables and decorated the rooms; it looks as if she's done her best to scare the young boy off. He who doesn't know which knife to use, in what order, he has no notion of etiquette. He holds his glass the wrong way, cupping the whole of his large hand in a crushing grip round the fragile bowl, and not with his fingers on the stem, the way my mother taught me to hold a glass. I can sit for hours staring at these photographs. Truly they're pictures of a drama: the young girl risks losing her boyfriend for good, and she will have both parents against her, they will tighten their grip on her, firmer, harder, if the visit isn't a success. If she, this sixteen-year-old, doesn't succeed with tonight's impossible visit, if her parents get their own way and she breaks off this relationship, in favour of a better connection, a boy from a better family, well, that would have been the end of me; the photographs would still exist, somewhere or other, in a drawer, in another flat, I don't know where; but I'd never have been able to look at them.

I can't claim to have disliked my grandmother, but I've always hated snobbery and social airs; I can't bear people who attach more importance to name and position than anything else: if my grandmother had her way, I wouldn't have existed. There are certain names and addresses I simply can't endure; I turn breathless when they're mentioned, I feel myself becoming dizzy and sick as soon as the names are spoken, these surnames, these Bergen names, seem to stick in my gullet and expand, blocking all airways. It's as if these names threaten my existence. At the age of nineteen I fell in love with a girl from Kalfaret, one of the most select parts of Bergen. She was tall and dark with black hair and blue eyes; I think she resembled my mother. She came from one of the oldest and richest families in the city. I was invited to dinner to meet her parents, her mother had decorated and laid the table, which stood in the centre of the large room with its stupendous view over the city, over the streets and lights below. We sat round the dining table, mother, father, Anne, her two brothers and me. We had an *hors d'oeuvre* accompanied by white wine. We had cod and drank red wine; I ate in moderation and sipped my wine. I made conversation, but couldn't relax, my involuntary anxiety and queasiness annoyed me, it got worse and worse, I sat at the table answering one thing after the other, where did I live and who were my parents, what was I studying and what were my future prospects; her mother wanted to know everything, she asked about everything imaginable. We had pudding and drank port; I tried to concentrate on Anne, I sat looking at her all evening, at how lovely she looked in a black dress with a white knitted jacket across her shoulders. There were white tulips on the table. A cake dish and candlesticks of silver, little cakes with the coffee; I sat at the coffee table and felt the nausea filling my body, forehead sweating, hair damp, hands clammy; I stood up saying I needed to go to the toilet. I went to the loo, bent over the toilet bowl and vomited all the nuts and fish, blackberries and ham.

I sit at my desk looking at the photographs of that dinner at Torgallmenningen 7 and think how different it all might have been; if my father had been like me, if he'd gone to the toilet, thrown up his food and decided never again to set foot in that living room, visit that family, if he hadn't put up with all the humiliating enquiries, comments, the oppressive atmosphere and the heavy, stagnant air, the suffocating heat of the living room, if he hadn't endured all this but decided to break with my mother, his girlfriend, completely, well, if he'd been like me and done like me, I would never have existed. The photographs would have been there, in someone else's hands. It's not hard to imagine another man, the same age as me, with a different name, a better surname; he sits flipping through pictures of his mother. And there it is; the photo of the dinner at Torgallmenningen with Else Marie Johannessen sitting next to her first love, his name unknown or forgotten. Maybe this other author imagines that they don't suit each other; the refined girl and this youth wearing a suit with his large hands and coarse features. Maybe this man, too, loved his mother, had just recently lost her, and perhaps wanted to tell quite a different story.

SEPTEMBER

Who knows
if I myself
might be called
something other
than myself.

Inger Christensen

My father was christened Eivind Olsen. At the age of thirteen he was given the name Eivind Espedal Olsen, it was his mother's wish, she wanted him to have her own name in his. Now he took the name Eivind Espedal; I think he did it for my mother's sake, she didn't want to be called Olsen. She didn't want to live in a block of flats. And yet she moved into a block of flats, the young couple couldn't afford anything else. They moved into a flat on the tenth floor, it was supposed to be temporary; they lived in the block for fourteen years. On the same floor, in the same flat; I don't know why they didn't move, it couldn't simply have been lack of money, they were both working; it may be that they stayed where they were because of a certain caution, or fear, a fear of change; I recognize the same thing in myself. I should have moved long ago. The old house is ruining my already fragile health; the icy draughts from the windows, the dampness in the walls and the coldness of the floors, a blue mould-like bloom on the bare wooden boards of the bedroom. A musty odour of fungus and rotten woodwork, of dead insects and animals; it's as if Nature has taken up residence in the house and turned putrid indoors, as if autumn has moved in and dragged all her leaves across the bedroom floor; a tang of leaves and apples. A sour smell of loneliness and putrefaction when I awake. I'm alone too much. There's too much silence, a dearth of movement in the house. There's too much loneliness in the house. Too many rooms in the house. Too many empty rooms; too much that's dead about the house. The old house will be the end of me; I sleep badly at night. Feel cold during the day, suffer severe bouts of giddiness. One evening when I'd gone to bed early with a book, I suddenly couldn't see the letters on the page, I turned the page but the letters were still absent, or they came together in a thin, illegible script that filled the leaves with shadowy characters; it was like witnessing the birth of a new language, or the end of sight, its disappearance, sight disappeared in front of my very eyes; I could no longer read books. In the morning I rummaged through the boxes of books under the bed and found a pair of glasses that had belonged to my mother, a pair of large, oval spectacles with wide, coloured plastic frames, the lenses covered the upper portion of my face and enabled me to see again, not fully and in focus, but enough to sit at my typewriter and read what I'd written on the page. My mother hated the flat in that block. The name Espedal was indeed on the door, and not Olsen, but that wasn't good enough for my mother, she wanted to move. During all the fourteen years she lived in the building, she wanted to go. When she got home from work at the hospital, the lift smelt of urine, someone had peed in the corner of the cramped cage, it was a daily occurrence, she pressed the button marked ten, it lit up. She stood in the corner of the overfilled lift, squashed by the bodies of strangers who pressed around her ever tighter as more people crowded in. She tried to make herself smaller, stood on tiptoe and felt the air being squeezed out of her, she lost her arms and legs, she lost her breath and hung there unconscious between the bodies in the lift. It was obvious to the street's residents that she didn't belong there, she stuck out. She didn't talk to the other women in the block, didn't say hello but walked past, as if she were too good to be where she was, in Skytterveien, on the tenth floor, why did she live there? She had no head for heights and was frightened of dogs. She always wore expensive clothes, her own special style; it was as if she were compensating for the unpretentious address on the tenth floor with exclusive clothes, she made up heavily and constantly changed hairstyles, she used hairpieces. She was blonde and sometimes brunette, her hair was piled up or hung in a black ponytail behind her as she went out of the door in the morning, it was eight o'clock, she was off to work. She stood in the corridor waiting for the lift. It arrived from the thirteenth floor, and when she opened the lift door, there was a dog inside. A black Dobermann, sitting in the corner of the lift, at the feet of its owner, who was holding the dog's leash. She opened the lift door and stared at the dog which pricked up its ears and got up, she smelt of hairspray and perfume. There, there, it's not dangerous; she let go of the lift door and backed away, walked to the stairs and stood there looking down at the ninth floor landing. She couldn't manage the stairs and she didn't dare take the lift, it was like being a captive in your own home, on the tenth floor, she was imprisoned in the block of flats where she lived.

Sometimes when she came home, all the mailboxes had been burnt. Four rows containing forty-two named boxes; someone had poured petrol or paraffin through the slits and set fire to the whole lot, names and post. At other times when she got home, the flat would be occupied by children, her own and some from the third and ninth floors; we'd be playing a sort of football game, or running from room to room and hiding in her wardrobes and clothes cupboards. She'd rigged up a kind of alarm in front of the balcony door, nylon thread with bells and clappers of wood that would sound a warning if any of us opened the door on to the small balcony; she imagined how one of us, how I, might climb the low railing and fall over the railings and plummet the ten storeys to the asphalt below. The flat had a view of the sea. From the balcony we could look at the city and the surrounding

mountains, the islands and the fjord that ran out
between Olsvik and the island of Askøy; a mouth, or
opening leading to the skerries and the ocean. In the
evenings, when cloud and darkness descended on the
city and its mountains, the view became a dense, black
wall that shut us in; we saw the tiny lights from the
houses beyond as stars in an all-encompassing sky; it
erased land and water which dissolved and became a
dark, mobile mass with pricks of light, it was as if we
lived high up in the air. We hung there between earth
and sky, a little illuminated abode among other lights
in the black heavens; the lights went out, one by one,
it was time to go to bed.

The lights went out, outside and in, the lights in the
houses and the light in the living room, in the hall and
in the bedroom, it was dark. Totally black. Not even
a strip of light under the door. No light from the window, no moon, no stars, only those thick brown vel-
vet curtains that smelt of dust, that smelt of earth. It
was like being buried in bed; I called out to my
mother. I could hear the noise of the lift, hauled by its
cables and motor, or was my room going down;
slowly, almost imperceptibly, being lowered down a

shaft that went down past all the floors, down to the basement and into the ground; I could hear it. How my bed was being lowered on strong cables towards that open hole in the earth, sinking down in the darkness; I called out to my mother. Her room was at the front of the house, my room was at the back, between us was a world of dark rooms. We were separated by a nocturnal world populated by dark lamps and old furniture, a terrifying chair, the brown sofa with arms that smelt of forest. During the day, from my room on the tenth floor, I could see right into the forest. At night I heard the wind in the trees, I heard the birds and other animals, sometimes it was like sleeping outside, under an open sky, I lay unprotected and surrounded by the noises of the forest, the darkness of the forest; I lay in the middle of the forest and didn't dare go to sleep. I called out to my mother. We inhabited two separate worlds at night. Between us was a great, dark forest and a great, dark living room where small creatures or beings squeezed under the chairs and tables, under the sofa and bookcases, wherever there was a gap for them to force their way in and curl up, only to swarm out and swell and inflate themselves so that they could gobble up anyone who tried to move in the living room at night. I could hear them, screaming and howling, did it come from the living room or the forest? I called out to my father. He came to my door immediately, opened it softly and came quietly into the room. He stood by my bed, bent down and kissed my cheek. He stroked my hair. He straightened my duvet and switched on the bedside lamp, draped a white shirt over the shade so that I could lie in the half-light: then, at last, I could sleep.

Sometimes at night, a figure would be standing in my room; I wasn't scared, but lay there motionless in bed, not opening my eyes, trying to look through my eyelids, which I slowly and cautiously opened a crack, so narrow that I couldn't tell if what I saw was on the inside or the outside of my eyes; was it a dream, or could I really see her in the doorway? She came into the room, gliding through the darkness and stopped by my bedside. She stood at the foot of my bed and looked at me. That was all, just stood there and looked. Then I heard a sigh, it came from my mother, she sighed. I wanted her to lie down on the bed next to me, but she drifted away from the bedside and out of the room, as silently as she'd come; what did she

want? Why had she stood by my bed at night looking
at the child that had grown up; it was too late now,
too late to say anything to the boy, too late to try to
comfort him in the dark, protect him from the things
he was scared of, the dark, the forest, the living room,
death, everything. It was too late, or was it? She vanished from the room, and I lay in bed with eyes wide
open; I could clearly see the bedside table and the window above the foot of the bed. Where was I? I was in
my bedroom in the house at Askøy; I lay in darkness
as usual, waiting for the fear to release its grip and for
drowsiness to gain a hold, like an anaesthetic, so that,
at last, I could sleep.

She woke me early in the morning, she was on her way
to work and had made my breakfast and packed my
school lunch which I fetched from the kitchen; I ate
in bed. I stayed in bed as long as I could, often I would
get up just so I could go to bed again; I sprinted out
to the kitchen and picked up my breakfast, carried it
back on a tray which I placed on the duvet, sat up in
bed supported by pillows and ate the slices of bread
and the pieces of fruit as I read a book. I was alone in
the flat. I could hear sounds from the people who

lived in the flats above and below and next door; it was as if the walls and ceiling and floor of my bedroom were thick membranes through which the noises and movements of neighbouring flats penetrated and took up residence in the room where I lay; there was a girl just behind the bedstead, close by my right ear; I could almost hear her whispering. There was a dog on the left of the room below my desk, it was eating, like me, and like me the dog enjoyed racing through the rooms, perhaps it was frightened, perhaps it was alone. In an hour's time I would set out for school, I only had to get up, go out to the bathroom and dress. My mother had left out my clothes, things she'd made herself, a suit-like uniform, brown trousers with a crease and a brown jacket with light brown buttons, it was dangerous to wear in the street, dangerous in the street in front of the blocks of flats, and all the way to school, but once I arrived in the classroom I was safe. My mother had had me moved into another class, away from the problem Skytterveien class and into a class with children from the detached houses of Biskopshavn. It was a dangerous move, but I managed it well; I learnt to fight and to win fights. I enjoyed living in Skytterveien. My mother wanted to move. As soon as possible. I don't know why we stayed there, perhaps we were short of money, perhaps there were various reasons; my father didn't want to move, and I certainly didn't want to, we stayed on. I lay in bed for as long as I could. Half an hour before school began, I leapt out of bed, ran into the bathroom and dressed rapidly. I took the lift down and walked quickly into the street, jogged past the low-rise blocks and the play area, past the Co-op and the football ground; I ran the whole way to school. It was all this running that saved me, that saved my uniform; I got safely there and back, not a scratch on me, not the slightest rent in my jacket or trousers.

The first time I fell in love was with a boy from the second floor, he was the youngest of five brothers. The Saars brothers, as we called them; at first I thought they were a family of gypsies, the brothers had swarthy complexions and jet black hair, they were always dirty and wore tattered clothes. Their clothes smelt of shit and piss; I could smell it as I stood pressed against the brothers in the lift or when one of them walked past in the street, they all stank, apart from him, the youngest, Helge, he didn't smell, or rather he smelt nice; I learnt that when he suddenly hurled himself at me, the nice smell of hair and earth and skin. He had a dark, girlish face with large, brown eyes and thin arched eyebrows which gave him an open, intense look, a melancholy look, I can say this now with hindsight but back then, when I looked at him, he only made me uneasy. His hair was long and curly, wild and unkempt hair that hung down over his face and hid it; he blew it away with his mouth. The long hair that fell to his shoulders and hung in a mane down his back, over the denim jacket he always wore. Tight trousers and wornout shoes, he never tied the laces, they just trailed behind him as he walked. He moved with long, quick strides as if he were always busy, he had nothing to do. He paced restlessly up and down the street, alone, on the lookout for bother or trouble. If nothing turned up, he'd make trouble himself; he'd break into a basement storage area, or he'd set fire to all the mailboxes, or he'd piss in the lift; I think that was him, I know it was. I'd follow him at a distance. There was something bestial and dangerous about him, he fought like an animal. If he were attacked, he bit as hard as he could, or he'd tug and tear at hair, like a girl, he scratched and punched, kicked and spat, it was impossible to win against him, he'd never give in. Sometimes he attacked without warning, it was as if something burst or exploded inside him, he struck out wildly and kicked at the groin and stomach, he aimed kicks at the head and wouldn't stop until his opponent lay motionless on the ground. It seemed almost as if he were standing over his prey ready to leap on it and sever the jugular with his teeth. I don't know what drove him, wildness and impulse, an instinct, perhaps an injury, perhaps his brothers had maimed him. Most people in the street were frightened of him and avoided him, he was generally on his own. He was standing alone on the flagstones outside the Co-op, the shop was closed, but there was a telephone box next to it, down the steps to the right of the concourse, he was standing smoking a cigarette. A cigarette end he'd found in the street. I saw him go into the telephone box and come out again. Lift and replace the receiver. I'd got off the bus, was walking up the hill from the bus stop. I'd been to a dancing class. I was forced to go to it. Twice a week. I was forced to go in black, shiny shoes, and a navy blue sailor suit which I concealed beneath a duffel coat, on Tuesdays and Thursdays. A black fur cap, which had flaps that could be tied over the crown, or under the chin when it was cold, it was cold, November. The day before my birthday. I was almost thirteen, we were the same age, we were in parallel classes, he stood on the flagstones and sucked on a cigarette butt. Got any coins? he asked. A couple of kroner pieces? he asked. I searched my pockets. Nothing. A banknote, but I couldn't pull that out of my pocket, the paper crackled. Got any notes? he asked. I shook my head. Nothing. No money, I lied. He said nothing, just stood there watching me lie. You won't be able to change it, I said. He laughed. Got smoke in his lungs and began coughing. Is it a hundred? he asked. I shook my head. So it's a tenner, he said. Lend it to us till tomorrow, will you? he asked. I can't, I said, it isn't mine. Whose is it? he asked. I didn't reply. I couldn't reply. I couldn't say: It's my mother's. I couldn't say: I've promised to give it back to her. If you don't know whose it is, then it's mine, he said abruptly. I need it, he said. I was ready now; he would attack. I looked around, to see if there was anyone in the vicinity, no one. Lights in the windows, lights on the tenth floor; I'd make a run for it. Just as I was about to take off, he launched himself at me. He wrapped his arms around my duffel coat and tried to get me down. I was surprised at how careful he was, perhaps he thought it would be easy, he got me in a hold and tried to throw me, but I pushed him away, shoved him off. Then he rammed his head as hard as he could into my chest, I fell backwards taking him with me. I got on top of him and planted myself on his chest, pinned his arms and tried to hold him firmly. At that moment he lifted his head, opened his mouth and bit at my crotch, at my scrotum. He bit, I felt his teeth through the material of my trousers, a frightful pain, I screamed and drove my knee at the biting mouth with all my strength, the back of his head hit the asphalt. It was really an accident, perhaps he was unconscious, I hit him in the face as hard as I could. He closed his eyes and offered no resistance. I went on hitting him and banged his head against the ground, again and again. Then I noticed that he was bleeding from the temple, there was blood in his hair and on the asphalt, I released him and stood up. He lay there, that frightened me more than anything, I ran as fast as I could towards the high-rise block, went up in the lift and let myself in, shouted for my father, I needed help, and no one else could help me but my father.

My father took me away from school, sent me to his mother in Michael Krohnsgate. I was to stay away for the rest of November and the beginning of December, right up to the Christmas holidays if necessary, my father would take care of the Saars family, as he put it. I didn't know what that meant, how he'd manage it; I still feel fear each time the name Saars comes into my head, the Saars family, Edgar Saars, occasionally I see one of the brothers in town by chance, Sigurd or Ove, and immediately I feel the old dread, the same fright, as if time were suspended and had vanished completely; I'm thirteen and being sent to my grandmother's in Michael Krohnsgate. My father would take care of the Saars family, I was sent away to his father and mother, it was as if we'd changed places; I was back in his youth. I was to live in his childhood home. His mother was, for a few months, my mother, I was, involuntarily, her son. She treated me like a son. In the next few months I became a different person; I knew what he'd felt, the other boy, my father.

I slept in my father's bed. I was awoken by his mother, she stood at the bedside and held out a cup of hot coffee-milk. He used to drink his milk with a drop of coffee in it, she would say, or: Now you hurry out to the kitchen and get dressed. I've heated water in the big saucepan, it's on the ring. And then you must go off to school, it's almost eight o'clock. I'm not going to school, I said. Oh, yes, I'd forgotten, you've got a sort of holiday, she said.

At night I'd get into bed behind the curtain she'd rigged up in the dining room, it was the only room with a stove, a coke stove that she kept going during the day, I heard it crackle at night. There was no hot water in the flat, the toilet was down the passage, the bathroom in the basement. I'd hear her come up the back stairs and into the kitchen to undress. There was a wardrobe in the corridor outside the kitchen, where her dresses and underwear, nightclothes and stockings were kept. She'd open the dining room door gently, pull the curtain aside and kiss me goodnight.

In the mornings we had breakfast together in the kitchen. She spoke of her father who'd worked on the railway, of her mother who'd died, and of Thea who'd moved into their house in Inndalsveien. She spoke of her sister Margit, and of her first meeting with her lover in the hut below Løvstakken, how he'd saved her. We lived together, got married and had a son, your father, she said. She talked away, bringing out the same stories over and over again, but each time a new detail was added, a new story, it wove itself into the others like a new thread in a great embroidery: her family tapestry. It hung there, unseen, on the kitchen wall, a large embroidered tapestry with characters she'd invented, landscapes as she recalled them, small studies of rooms and furniture which were sketched and woven together in her imagination; a tapestry of scenes from working life and family life, with streets and houses, a long, narrow street with blocks of brick buildings and children playing, and in the background, behind all the changing motifs, behind all the narratives, far away, like a miniature in the great, colourful weft: a picture of the harbour. Quayside cranes and shipyards, boats and factories, workers and seamen, small characters stitched in place between the buildings and the sea; I could see the same image from the flat where we were sitting, from the dining-room window; it was as if she'd put me into the tapestry she was weaving, I was being painstakingly woven into her story, the whole of my background and history, and gradually, too, my present, she cut it out and sewed it into this tapestry of motifs that resembled the ones I saw every single day from the dining-room window.

On Sundays the whole family gathered, either in
Michael Krohnsgate or in Torgallmenningen. Elly
Alice and Alfred, Erling and Aagoth, Eivind and Else
Marie and her sister Unn. We sat at the plain dining
table in Michael Krohnsgate, or round the lavishly laid
one in the dining room in Torgallmenningen. I'd just
learnt that my mother was pregnant, I'd been told
we'd be moving. My parents had been to look at a terraced house in Øyjordsveien, they'd put in an offer,
my maternal grandfather was willing to help them
with a loan; they talked about it round the dinner
table. The terraced house was no more than ten minutes' walk from the blocks of flats in Skytterveien, the
distance was small, but great, as I saw it; it was the distance from the Saars family in Skytterveien to the
posh family names in Øyjordsveien, from my friends
in the street to the enemy in the villa district. This was
where I was moving to, only to a terraced house ad-
mittedly, but still in enemy lines, I was moving into
enemy country. My mother said I would stay at the
same school, in the same class, she thought it a piece
of good news, but it was bad news. There won't be
much difference, she said, but I knew the difference
would be colossal. Better to move to the other end of

town, or to a different city, better to move to a different country. Now it would be clear to my friends, and to the boys in the street, what I really was, what I'd always been: an upstart.

And today: the first of the cold weather. A cold wind, it blows right through the house. We are awoken early by the sudden cold and the strong wind lashing rain and hail against the windowpanes; she sleeps with her window open and there's a thin, white coating of hail on the duvet at the foot of her bed.

It's colder inside the house than out of doors; a new, old chill, as if autumn has overwintered indoors, it's survived spring and summer, and now re-emerges in full vigour inside the house, outside it's still late summer.

The twigs of rowanberry in the big vase on the desk have lost their leaves and berries; they lie red and split on the table, as if September were one month inside and another out: the rowanberries and apples hang red and ripe in the clear garden sunlight.

It's autumn in the house.

The cut roses curl their withered petals in towards the centre of the flower so that the brown petal edges form a new pattern of old flower in the middle: a new flower, the withered flower.

Outside things mimic those within.

Autumn begins in the bedroom and migrates slowly down to the living room and into the workroom where it's noted; it clings like a scent to the clothes, like a heavy, ripe fruit somewhere between the lungs and the heart, before moving on, out of the house, out into the garden, out into the apple trees and flowers. There are three apples on the writing table. It will be several weeks before the skins and colours of the apples on the tree will take on the same unnatural, lonely sheen as the half-rotten apples on the table.

And today: a letter in the mailbox. Folded in among the newspapers. The postman wanted to protect the letter from the rain and wrapped the papers around the envelope; it's not difficult to imagine the newspapers and the letter getting soaked, if I didn't fetch the post, if it continued to rain, a heavy cloudburst, continual rain, the newspapers would become soggy, and the letter too; it would be illegible.

It's happened before; it rained, I didn't collect the post.

The birds are flying in an arrowhead formation, it looks like a huge wing or the outline of a lily leaf, a gentle curve, a soft bow in the sky shooting the birds in a straight line across the lily pond.

The birds' migration reflected in the water, as if the birds are flying through the open flowers.

The birds are flying south in a straight line above the pond and the stand of mailboxes nailed up between the bushes and the dog roses. The flowers push up between the boxes, an orangey-red tangle of hips and roses, the petals dropping from the flowers and forming a thin line in front of the mailboxes. There are birds in the dog rose hedge and the berry bushes; magpies and thrushes, sparrows and tits, they gulp red currants and black currants, gooseberries and hips. Occasionally there are one or two rose petals in the mailbox.

A letter. Among the newspapers. A white envelope, addressed by hand. A handwritten letter. I read the newspapers first. Then I read the letter. It's a personal letter, practically a threat, he writes: It will be necessary for you to move out. The house must be vacated within two weeks. I must, on behalf of my daughter, request that the house be sold.

And today: my child, my daughter is ill. She arrives home early from school with a temperature, lies down with her clothes on, pulls the duvet over her; I run down to the shop, buy lemonade and digestive biscuits. When I get back, she's gone to sleep. I sit on her bed and look at her, just a slight temperature, only a touch of flu. Her face is flushed, her brow hot, her hair damp; suddenly I start crying, I just can't stop. It's only a touch of flu, a slight temperature, a little queasiness; I open the window, tuck the duvet around her. I don't know why, but I clean her room, I wash the floor with soft soap and wipe the shelves. I tidy her things. Hang up her clothes. Then I clean the living room and the bathroom. I hoover the carpets. Change the water in the bucket and wash the stairs. After that, I wash the windows. When at last I'm exhausted, I go up to her bedroom, sit by the bed and wait for her to wake up. My child, my daughter, is sick and I'm her mother.

I sit at my writing table, tie my hair into a ponytail. My hands have altered. The nails have got longer; I want to write like a woman.

The way the flowers wither and the roses bend forward
and break   Isn't the autumn a fall
Falling   red
The tallest flower   white and dead
At night   At night the rose loses
                                                the light
extinguishes the flower   and turns black
and turns white   or red
Yellow and deeper yellow   or lighter yellow
like the lamplight and the lamp   the reflection of
                                                light

in the window   the darkness
that reflects the flowers   in the autumn
How the darkness mimics   the rose
the pattern of the folds   petal above petal
and the rose petals turn darker   at the edges
a September-brown colour   withered
eating away at life   at the beginning
and the end   towards the middle   and the end

This day: I don't know
whether I like it or not,   whether to be sad
whether to be happy,   this ninth of September day

It's   not a day
a day like all others   without you
without you towards the end   and me

The roses too will turn black.
The desk lamp will be turned off.
It will turn dark.
It will turn cold.

The best would be if there were snow,
an early snowfall to cover the flowers
before the petals fall.
The best would be if you could see
those white flowers from the window,
and it was warm in the room.
A warmth from the fireplace, from the birch logs
which you sawed and split back in April.
The best would be if the snow were washed away.
You could still sit in the garden,
what if it were Tuesday; it could be
your birthday.
The best would be if you had company,
an unexpected visit.
Such as your dearest friends, those closest to you.
A special guest. You hadn't invited him.
The best would be if he didn't come.
For everything to go on as before, before he came.
For everything to be normal.
For this autumn to be a lovely autumn.
The best would be if it were a lovely winter

and a mild spring. For the apple to blossom in April,
with the daffodils and crocuses.

Isn't it strange how the same petals

that push out the white, small, rose-like flowers,

will transform those flowers into apples?

The apples will grow, almost out of nothing.

They'll grow and turn ripe, red apples with streaks
of yellow in their redness.

If only you could eat the apples.

Some of the apples ought to remain on the boughs.

In the autumn you could see how heavy the apples
were.

You could see them fall.

The apples fall towards the grass, they lie there in a
circle

around the tree.

Magpies and thrush come and peck at the apples, suck
the juice out of them and eat the fruits' flesh.

Some of the apples shrink. Some of the apples turn
to earth.

Isn't it strange that those same apples

that lay in the grass around the tree,

are suddenly gone one day.

Can you understand it? Do you understand this miracle

of the apples?

It's repeated every year.

Every spring and every autumn.

April and September, each and every year.

The best would be if you didn't think of this,

this vigorous, lovely life which continues year after year.

The birds and the flowers.

The house and the garden.

The girls playing. They're running in and out of the garden gate.

This autumn and next autumn; I know you thought about them,

about what would happen to them, what they'd look like,

whether they'd have short hair or long hair,

whether I'd cut it or not.

Whether they'd look like you,
whether they'd remember you
or not.
The best would be if the winter were mild.
The best would be if the snow were washed away.
The girls might play in the garden,
building a kind of hut among the rhododendrons,
fully furnished with a small table and chairs.
They lay the table with plastic plates and cups,
there will be tea and buns.
Just the way you liked it.
They're obviously expecting a visit.

Another letter in the mailbox. Between the newspapers. I read the papers first, then I read the letter.

How the house collapses, falls, the structures fail and the windows shatter, the roof snaps in the middle and plunges towards the floor; an internal avalanche that leaves the facade standing without rooms. Without doors and stairs, without furniture. The facade stands for a few minutes, before disintegrating under the weight of destruction, from the thought that we'll be moving out.

How the house comes crashing down as we sit eating dinner; the walls buckle and crumble vertically, bring-

ing with them roof tiles which smash the interior, first
on the upper storey, the beds and bedroom; we watch
the roof opening and breaking in a rain of stone and
wood, beams and glass that smash the upstairs floor,
tearing down the bedroom and the girls' room almost
simultaneously in one fall to the ground. The windows
shatter and the doors burst open. The staircase breaks
step by step and leans at a new angle that strikes the
door of the workroom. The lights go out and flash
blue, electric sparks by paper and curtains, a terrible
light, we see how the grey light flies through the
rooms which aren't rooms any more, but square holes
full of ash and dust. We're sitting at the dining table in
the living room; I try to tell her, not knowing what
words to use, but I say it: We must get ready to move
house.

An unlooked for gift: my sister and her husband have
bought a new caravan, I take over their old one; a
small two-wheeler shaped like a curved home, with a
door and two windows.

I get the van moved from Åsane to Askøy: Jan Kåre
and I push the small caravan through the garden gate,

pull it across the lawn and position it right next to the house, to the left of the front door, beneath the copper beech tree. The front, with its door and bow window, towards the gate and the old view which now becomes new. I run an extension cable from the house to the van, this provides electricity and light in my new, mobile workroom. The afternoon is spent dismantling the plastic table and all the unnecessary fittings in the caravan; I carry in a wooden writing table, a leather chair and two lamps. Take out the cupboard doors and line the new shelves above the writing table with books. In the evening I carry out my typewriter and writing materials. Glasses and coffee cups. Some plates and cutlery for the little kitchen; there is a gas bottle under the kitchen worktop, a two-ring gas stove and a gas heater next to the toilet, a hand-pumped shower and a small wash basin, mirror and cabinet on the wall. I fetch my washing things, a duvet and a pillow, clean bed linen, and make a bed. I get into bed, close my eyes and am suffused with a new sense of happiness, a totally new feeling of freedom; the caravan is stationary, attached to the house and the garden, but it's not hard to imagine it on the move.

Sunlight wakes me; it strikes the flowers on the writing table, they shine, white chrysanthemums. A coffee cup, an ashtray, my pen and sheets of paper, lying in a pile on the table. White. My notebooks, black. Black covers of thicker paper, hand-sewn down the spine. Handwritten lines, page after page, book after book, twelve books in all; the notebooks, the outlines of a novel. An anglepoise lamp. Grey metal, a yellowish light. The typewriter, black keys, white letters. A pile of books, a photograph. Three apples, lying on the writing table, rotting. The skins shrivel, form dark blotches with black centres. Small scars on the skin which come together around the stalk; the broken link between fruit and tree. A chair, a red cushion on the chair. A Turkish carpet on the floor. Yellow, flower-patterned curtains framing the window above the bed; a bunk with a mattress and white sheet, white bed-clothes, a white pillow with an embroidered white rose.

The first night in the caravan; I'm awoken by the sunlight and the sound of the birds. Blackbird and magpies, it's not difficult to imagine the caravan parked in a forest. Or on the edge of one; a wall of trees, naked, wet, as after a shower of rain. A framed picture on the wall above the bed, a copy of a painting: *The Origin of the World*. Gustave Courbet's picture in its original dimensions, 46 x 55 cm; it appears to be the precise reproduction, and the exact size, of a female sexual organ.

I'm not going anywhere, don't want to go anywhere; I won't get anywhere. And yet; this shifting to a caravan is a big move, a minor journey; I follow the roads on the map that's hanging on one wall, and the caravan moves off, first to the city and its streets, then by boat to England and some of the places I remember from books and photographs: Halifax, Sheffield, Wiltshire, Hampstead and south towards Thomas Hardy's Wessex; the spot, near Melchester, with the great stone slabs, Stonehenge, where Tess was discovered asleep as the sun penetrated the stones and woke her: it'll soon be broad daylight, the caravan is rolling on through the tunnel under the Channel, into France; I visit Peter Handke just outside Paris, in No Man's Bay.

Those beautiful forests outside Chaville. Near where the Forest of Rambouillet turns into the Forest of Versailles, a belt of forest, the unfolding trees with new shoots of hazel and chestnut, planted in alleys which bisect woods of birch, white, thin trunks, shining like snow, darkened by the shadows of older trees, beech and oak.

Fontainebleau. An opening in the forest; a clearing, or a garden, lilies and iris, anemones and peonies, violet and red, surrounded by lilac and bird cherry. A stone-built house with red roof tiles. Large windows. Window boxes. A balcony. The house of Marguerite Duras at Neauphle-le-Château, it's next to the school, sheltered by hedges and trees, a large pond and an overgrown garden which encloses the house in a thicket of bushes and flowers. I park the caravan right by the Duras house, as I lie here I can see the lamps in the windows, they're like my mother's lamps; dark, thick linen lampshades on feet of china and wood, plastic and glass, they're all over the house.

I can manage all right on my own.

All diary jottings are declarations of independence.

I can't manage on my own.

Notes about April: snowdrops and crocus, white anemones and coltsfoot, then cress and dandelion, daffodils and tulips; these are the first flowers in my mother's garden.

In April my mother caught a cold, a light cold, it lasted the whole of April and wasn't gone by May, nor by June, and not by July, not by August, and in September her cold was still there, in her body, it wouldn't loosen its hold.

April, May, June, July, August, hot, lovely months, they were killing my mother.

In September she went to the doctor, she complained of a cold and learnt that she was seriously ill.

Everyone said it was one of the best, one of the hottest and finest summers we'd had.

The rhododendron was flowering in April, first the white flowers, then the pink and yellow ones, and as always, every year, the vibrant red ones last, they opened like great, red wounds.

In April Agnete and I parted, for the eighth or ninth time but this time it was final, it was over, it was over between us.

It was the end of spring, the beginning of summer. My mother had already begun to die.

In April my mother was strong and demanding, at times stubborn, her usual self, but in June she was thinner and weaker, she was quieter than normal, in July she was almost a different person, and by September she had the mark of death on her.

In April she cut and dyed her hair as was her custom. After work she lay on the patio, in the sun, with a bottle of water into which she'd put some sea salt, she lay in the sun and poured the water over herself, to get a better skin colour. A deeper skin colour. Her hair was short and black, her skin dark and beautiful, like the skin of a young girl, almost.

In September she was old. It happened so quickly that we found it hard to believe, perhaps we shut our eyes and behaved as if everything were normal: from then on we no longer saw her. She vanished before our eyes.

In April the first snowdrops appeared in the garden. Then the crocuses, violet, white. At the end of the month there were coltsfoot and dandelions, the ground was covered in cress. We received the usual injunction not to cut the grass, only when the cress had withered did my father fetch the lawnmower from the cellar and mow it.

In April spring and autumn arrived with full force.

In April the flowers burst from the ground, the birds arrived, the wagtail and blue tit and song thrush came, the great tit and blackbird came, and the owl came; it had never come before.

In April the birds found their trees. The wood pigeon came, the sparrows came, the woodpecker came and the terrible jay; we couldn't sleep at night, in the morning, when the light came in, it was impossible to sleep, madness came, spring's madness; it was screeched out at night and in the morning.

The owl took over the beech tree outside the bedroom windows, a large, dark, cat-like bird that suddenly launched itself from its perch, it was unnatural, as if a dog had suddenly learnt to fly, it opened its wings and glided past our windows.

I'd moved back home, back to my boyhood bedroom in Øyjordsveien. Agnete and the two girls moved to an old house, which she'd bought, on Askøy. It turned into a long and hot summer, one of the hottest for many years; the summer reached into spring and into autumn, spreading its branches in all directions, just like a tree, first the white flowers broke out like snow on the ends of the green buds, and the next moment, or so it seemed, the apples hung from the boughs.

It happened so quickly that we found it hard to believe, perhaps we shut our eyes, we shut our eyes, and when we opened them again, the autumn and spring were over, we'd lost the summer.

In September Agnete celebrated her birthday in the Askøy house with two children and two men; we sat in the garden and grilled chops and sausages, ate a piece of the cake with its forty-one candles, they were planted in the white cream and covered the entire cake; Agnete blew them all out in one great puff, it was a sinister omen, an awful sight.

In September my mother lost her hair.

'In the chronology of the rose, fading attracts the most comment.'

In September the first leaves dropped from the trees. The bees deserted the rhododendrons and roses, the flowers were sucked dry and empty. The petals hung like thin shells on stalks that were losing their flowers, petal by petal. The bees left the flowers and attached themselves to the plum trees, hundreds of yellow insects sucking at the plums, opening them and drawing the juice from the fruit before flying back to the hives that stood in blue and white rows on our neighbour's ground.

We heard the bees' hum at night, like electricity, a sharp, malicious sound that kept us awake; it seemed that the night wanted to deprive us of sleep.

In September: it was impossible to sleep. On some nights I heard my mother cry out in bed, sudden, loud screams; I don't know if she was awake or asleep, if she'd suddenly seen something that lay in store for her. In the mornings she sat at the bottom of the stairs smoking cigarettes; we caught the smell of tobacco that flowed through her and wafted up the stairs and into the bedrooms where we lay wakeful and afraid.

She had to stop smoking, we forced her to. A nicotine patch was stuck on her chest, but she continued to smoke, in secret, we smelt it in the toilet and the basement, and after she'd had a cigarette, she'd stagger across the living room, sometimes she'd walk in or out of the wrong door, or she'd sit down on a chair that wasn't there, we found her lying on the floor. There's nothing wrong with me, she said.

She smoked furtively, she was fourteen or fifteen, we were her parents and life was running backwards in her; she became younger and younger each month, soon we'd have to start nursing her.

In December, just before Christmas, I moved into a flat in Danmarksplass, two rooms and a kitchen in a caretaker's apartment on a factory site. I was never able to furnish the rooms, I was never able to do anything, except lie on a mattress on the floor, drinking cartons of wine, morning, noon and night.

I tried to write, but couldn't produce anything. I wanted to write about my mother but couldn't.

I still can't. I want to write about my mother's death but I can't. It's the first time I've come up against such an obvious and insurmountable barrier; I'm unable to cross it, I don't want to. I knew nothing of this barrier until I encountered it just now, as I wrote the sentence: Soon we'd have to start nursing her. There it ground to a halt, the language stopped; I had to get up from my writing table and light a cigarette, I'm close to breaking down.

I'm lying in the caravan, it's parked next to the house on Askøy, from where I lie I can see the windows of the house, they're lit up, it's the light from the lamps I inherited from my mother; I've put the lamps in the living room and in the bedroom, in the work room, on the desk. 'Writing hasn't helped me,' wrote Peter Handke in his book about his mother: *A Sorrow Beyond Dreams*. She committed suicide aged fifty-one, the last sentence of the book reads: 'I'll write about all this later in more detail.' But Peter Handke hasn't.

In February my mother was admitted to Haukeland Hospital. An extra bed was wheeled into her room, my father occupied it during the day and I at night, we took turns lying next to her. She died in April. We had lain next to her, day and night, for almost two months; my father would go home just after I arrived, and I went home right after he came in the morning but on the day she died I went home a little before my father had appeared, I can't remember why but I think there was a gap of about half an hour between us, and in that interval she died. She died alone.

It's been decided, the house on Askøy is to be sold.

When you've been unhappy in a place long enough, it's sometimes the case that you're more strongly attached to that place than to any other: you can be weighed down by a perverse happiness that binds you more firmly to that house than to others; suddenly you don't want to move. Every day, right from the start, from that very first moment in the house on Askøy, I've wanted to get away, but now, after all these years, when I'm being forced to move, when at last I can go somewhere else, I don't want to, I don't want to move.

Each time we move, it's inescapable, we're forced to think about death: we're moving for the last time. We can't move any more but not even this last time is final; now we're going back to where we came from. I grew up on the tenth floor: in a sense I can say that I've never moved away, just further and further down; I've lived on the fourth floor, on the third floor, on the ground floor, and I'm writing this in a basement. I'm writing this in the basement at Øyjordsveien, about half a kilometre from where I grew up, in Skytterveien. I'm writing in the basement room, two metres below ground, literally underground, in the earth, beneath the lawn which I can see above me through the basement window, a small pane of glass looking out at the wall that encloses the small front garden.

My father and I shuttle back and forth between Ask and Øyjordsveien with a removal van; we move books and other necessities from one place to the other: a writing table, a chair. Beds, bedside tables, lamps. We empty one house and fill another, a house that's already full of childhood things and teenage things, of my mother's things, which we still haven't managed to throw away. Her clothes are in the wardrobes. Her books are on the shelves. Sometimes I think she's still here, that she might simply get up and put on the jeans and shirt that hang in the wardrobe, or that she might be lying in bed reading as usual. Perhaps she's reading one of the books on the bedside table. She's reading one of my books, she's surreptitiously removed one of the books from the pile and will put it back without me noticing. My father doesn't want her things thrown out or moved; never, not even for a day, in all the years and months and days she's been dead, has he come to terms with her death. I've never seen anything like it, such daily devotion to someone who's gone; I think he still clings to the possibility she might return. I'd expected his sorrow to diminish, that he'd see reason, and adjust to being alone, but he behaves as if she's still here; not, it's true, with the same fervour and intensity as formerly but still with enough conviction and force to need to relate to her; she can't be that far away, and if she's really never going to return, then he'll prepare to follow her.

He decides to move. My father moves into sheltered accommodation; a single room with kitchen and bathroom, a small hall. It's practically a waiting room with just enough space to lie in bed, just enough space to sit on the sofa and wait to be taken away to an even smaller place. I'm close to tears each time I leave him in that room, but he sits heroically in his armchair and waves me brusquely off. It's as if he's trying to say: I know, I know what you're thinking, Tomas, and perhaps your right, it's too soon, I shouldn't be here, not yet, but go home now and take good care of your daughter, she's the dearest thing we have.

The new, old home; I paint my old room pink, pink walls with a white ceiling, white cupboard doors, I pull up the carpet and sand the floor before painting the wood, board by board, with shiny, white paint. Then I place the writing desk by the window, a lamp on the table, put a bookshelf up and position her bed in the corner where my own bed stood: after school, in the evening, she can sit at her writing table and look out of the window; the view is the same, it is almost unchanged, but otherwise nothing is as it was before.

I don't know how I'm going to manage without my father, I daren't think about it, and yet I think about it all the time, in the morning when I wake up and in the evening: I won't manage without him. I must manage without him; in a few years he'll be gone, perhaps just at the moment my daughter moves out: one day, and although I'm prepared, it will be sudden, like tearing the floor away from underneath someone in a room, I'll be left standing in thin air, like a cartoon character flapping its arms to hold itself up and stop itself falling, concentrating; I must concentrate on not falling.

I must concentrate on writing. At first you write to get a book published, to be able to call yourself a writer, gradually you begin to write to earn money, you write to have work, and you write to write better, better and better books, never worse books, each book must be better than the last, it's a rule that makes it almost impossible to write books; an author, wrote Thomas Mann, is someone who finds it harder to write than anyone else. But after many years and a succession of books, you think less about the money and the books; writing has become a necessity, a necessity of life, you can't manage without your writing.

I reorganize the basement room, turn my mother's sewing room into a writing room, a workroom. In the corner where my mother sat at her sewing machine, I shall sit at my typewriter: I'll write a book about moving house.

We drove away from Skytterveien to Øyjordsveien, down the hill past the low-rise blocks and the Co-op, and up the hill towards the villas that stood on a rise with a view of the city's fjord and Askøy. It was a three-minute drive. My father had driven back and forth between the high-rise block and the terraced house in a van he'd borrowed from the factory; load after load. Load after load of furniture and clothes, it seemed as if the flat was inexhaustible, as if we'd hoarded all there was of consumer durables during the sixties and seventies; now my father made the last journey, in the newly purchased Saab, he drove the family home.

The terraced house lay right out on a shoulder of the mountain, on the edge of Øyjordsfjellet, there was a small copse below the terrace, a declivity of aspens and birches, they grew down towards the houses in Solbakken. Behind the house was a school garden, and the old farm buildings which were gradually hidden and enclosed by all the new housing that shot up in record time as the farmer sold one building plot after another in the years 1974 to1979. Our terrace was in four units: C, D, E and F. A and B were garages; we were to live in E; the E house had three storeys, basement, a middle storey with living room and kitchen, a small toilet, and on the first floor there were three bedrooms and a bathroom. I was given the biggest one, a relatively large room with a view of the school garden. My parents took the smallest bedroom, there was just enough space for a double bed, but the room had a large window, an opening on the sea, and that made it seem bigger, infinite, almost. My father set about tearing down the walls in the basement, it had four partitions which he wanted to turn into a living room, a television room, with wall-to-wall carpet, a bookcase, two mock-leather sofas, three chairs and a large table where my mother could have a sewing machine, a combined sewing and television room in the basement; that was how my father occupied himself after work. Christmas was coming. The new home had to be ready by Christmas Eve; we were to celebrate Christmas with the entire family in Øyjordsveien.

I had a green carpet put down in my room, and chose a dark blue colour for the walls. The mouldings and cupboards were painted white, a white ceiling, a large light fitted with a linen shade, it filled the room with a soft, yellow light which could be completely shaded from the outside by locking the door and drawing the heavy, light brown curtains, sewn by my mother. I placed the writing table in front of the window, with the bed next to it, two chairs and a bookshelf, that was all; that was how I arranged the room which was to resemble all the rooms I've ever lived in since the first one in Skytterveien. My mother bought and read books, lots of books, she had them on the bed and under the bed; stacks of books, which, after she'd read them, went on shelves, in the living room and in the basement. She read in bed, by the light of the bedside lamp; I could see her through the chink in the door on my way to the bathroom, she lay on the edge of the double bed wearing a small white cap, and glasses that magnified her eyes making her look like some alien from outer space, she resembled, as I only now realize, a Jewish rabbi, at any rate a man, with her black hair under the white skullcap, her large, pointed nose and her round eyes; I saw to my considerable alarm, once I reached the bathroom, that she looked like me.

I'd got her nose and mouth, as I saw from the bathroom mirror; I'd got her eyes, all that was missing was a few years and a pair of glasses, and it could have been me lying there in bed reading.

I borrowed her books as soon as she'd finished them, I stole into the bedroom and pulled the one she'd just read, out of the pile on the bedside table, exchanging it for the one I'd just read and hoping she wouldn't notice I was reading the same books as her. They were books about women and sexuality. She read, I read, books by Betty Friedan and Marilyn French, Suzanne Brøgger and Erica Jong, but during that first year at Øyjordsveien, she read *Martha Quest* by Doris Lessing, and this book made such an impression on me that for a while I dreamt I was a girl; I wanted to be one, a fifteen-year-old girl rebelling against her mother.

Martha Quest wanted to rebel against everything that was expected of her, that threatened to trap her into being something she didn't want to be; she didn't want to be like her mother. I didn't want to be like my mother, or my father; I couldn't be bothered to listen to all their nagging about homework and getting good marks and making something of myself. Martha wanted to live in a different way, in her own way, and I wanted to live like her, I identified with her, and was, for a few weeks before Christmas, a fifteen-year-old girl who wanted to rebel against her mother.

I went into town, took the bus from the School of Commerce to the city centre, past Skoltegrunnskaien with its terminal and boats to England, to Newcastle, every Saturday, as I'd discovered, today was Thursday; I got off the bus at Torgallmenningen and jogged to the bookshop in Strandgaten. I wanted to buy a map and some books. I wanted to buy a map of Britain and a couple of novels by Charles Dickens; I wanted to buy the map and the books and get home as quickly as possible. I walked straight back from the bookshop to the bus stop in Torgallmenningen. No bus; I had to wait, I was waiting for a Number 9 bus. Then two things happened, almost simultaneously; first, I caught sight of my maternal grandfather, he came walking down the street, a tall figure in a hat and coat, round glasses, black, shiny shoes, a stick that he swung in a mechanical and precise arc, it couldn't be anyone else, and yet to me he seemed alien, as if he didn't belong

to the street he was walking up, it seemed to me that
he came from far away, as if he'd strolled all that way
from a foreign country or a different age; I couldn't
connect this man to my family, or to myself, I was suddenly scared that he would bump right into me, that
he'd recognize me, and that I'd have to address
him, talk to him, what would I say? What would we
talk about? I would stand there tongue-tied and
ashamed and frightened, frightened of the unfamil-
iarity between us. Just at that moment the bus arrived,
and sitting at the back I saw Helge Saars and two of
his brothers. I'd been too preoccupied with my grandfather; now the brothers had spotted me before I
noticed them, they got up as one from their seats and
ran to the rear door. Helge banged on it so that the
driver would open up; the door opened, should I
shout for my grandfather? I certainly wanted to shout,
but what should I shout; Grandfather or Erling; I
didn't dare call out to him.

He walked past. Passed a few yards away from me; I
was forced to stand still, wanted to jump into the bus
as soon as the driver opened the front door, but a
powerful jerk yanked me out of the queue. I was slung

back against the shop windows at the bus stop. The
two brothers stood behind Helge, ready to take a hand
if I managed to get away, run; I didn't want to run, I
wanted to get it over, wanted to be rid of this fear that
had haunted me every day for weeks, months. Helge
began to lash out; I felt it as a kind of relief, at last, he
was beating away the fear, the coldness, the lump of
ice in my body, it evaporated and vanished; I felt only
warmth, warmth and the pain of the blows and kicks.
He kicked at my crotch and stomach, punched my
face and eyes, it happened so quickly that I hardly felt
the blows and he wouldn't stop, scratched and bit,
charged at me so that my head cracked against the
glass wall, one of the display windows, the glass went
bang and so did my head, a terrible bang in my head;
I lost my hearing and vision, and everything went
quiet and dark. I fell. It was as if I could see it all from
above, from a different place, I don't know where, perhaps it was just my imagination, I saw my body falling
and Helge continuing to kick at my head and chest;
someone's got to stop him, I don't know whether it was
a thought or a cry; they came running out of the shop
and managed to get me up, two female shop assistants,
and pulled me into the shop and supported me through

the premises, into the back room where there was a cloakroom. I was placed on a bench and fell to the floor. My mother often said: It was a pity you never got to know your grandfather properly, he would have enjoyed talking and arguing with you, he wrote, you know, songs and short stories, thousands of letters, your grandfather was artistic, and he would have liked to know that you're like him, that you've become like him, she said, that was just after he died, at Easter, but on Christmas Eve he sat at the dinner table and looked steadily at his grandchild who was all plastered and bandaged and sewn up so that he resembled no one else in his family; I think he was ashamed or irritated by this battered boy who could neither speak nor eat, and certainly I was nothing like him, my grandfather with his beautiful, white hair combed back in elegant waves and curls above the narrow face with its large eyes that stared at me as if I came from a different world, a dirtier and coarser world; he sat at the table with a white linen napkin pushed into his collar, dark suit, gold glasses, perhaps it was the glance of an old man who'd made a disquieting discovery; he didn't know his own family.

The meat was brought in, beer and aquavit was poured into glasses, my father tapped his knife on his crystal glass and made a short speech of welcome; a welcome to the new home in Øyjordsveien. Then he explained how some chums and I had tobogganed down the mountain, Øyjordsfjellet, down the pass at Schnitlerskaret, a lethal slope, I'd run straight into a tree and broken two ribs, smashed my mouth and damaged my teeth; and so Christmas Eve was begun with a lie and ended with the truth.

We raised our glasses.

I don't know if you remember, that first time, that first taste of alcohol, the way the liquid pricked your tongue and burnt inside your body, a heat or recognition of something you hadn't known about, as if something inside you had been waiting for this stuff, as if you identified the destruction at once, the moment you tasted the first drop, the first sip of spirits. We raised our glasses. It was the first time I'd been allowed alcohol. A small glass of beer with my food, perhaps they felt sorry for me because I had difficulty eating, my mouth and head hurt; I'd taken painkillers, and

now I was tasting beer and secretly trying a little aquavit, spirits; it pricked my tongue and burnt inside my
body like a good heat, a warm softness and peace that
spread internally, as if something had fallen into place,
something that had been missing, or was it something
that had been out of balance and came into equilib-
rium; I was impatient and couldn't wait until the guests
had gone, until my parents were in bed, I had to go
out into the kitchen and sample the cognac and the
whisky and a little of the port that had been bought
for the pudding and the cakes and the evening and the
night; my father would sit alone, after the guests had
gone, he liked to sit alone with the bottle, I knew that,
he liked drinking, and I didn't know that I had the
same predilection as him.

   I tasted the spirits and sat down again at the dining table, everything was better now; the snow lay like
cotton wool over the house and the terrace, a white
shelter that packed us into the living room; the warm
living room, the fire was lit; I sat there with strips of
plaster on my eyes and bandages around my chest,
cocooned in cotton wool and alcohol. Snow and
dresses, my mother's and grandmothers' dresses, red,
black, blue material that rustled and smelt of perfume

and cigarettes. I'd wanted a pair of boxing gloves. I got a new pair of pyjamas. Two books and a pair of shoes for winter. A white shirt, a leather cap, it didn't matter what I'd got; what I wanted most of all was for the guests to go home. I wanted to sit alone with my father. I wanted to talk to my father, drink with my father, and forgot that it was too soon, that I was too young, that what would become a habit still wasn't possible; the two of us sitting in the basement talking of things past; my mother, her parents, his parents, they were all gone. And that first Christmas in Øyjordsveien, we both of us, my father and I, wished that they'd go home, the whole family, so we could be alone, he and I, we wished them gone, but today, now they are all gone, we wish they were here, that they'd never left us alone.

My mother wore a red dress with a silver belt, a dark hairpiece tied in a topknot, large gold earrings and a white necklace on her brown skin; she used to sit under a sun lamp. Sometimes she was blonde, at other times her hair was reddish, or brown, but this evening, on Christmas Eve, it was black, and rolled into a topknot, which with her high-heeled shoes, made her taller than usual. We clasped hands around the Christmas tree. She was holding my hand; I bent suddenly towards her and kissed her naked shoulder. Tomas, she whispered looking at me: Good God, what a sight you are, I can smell it on you, you're turning out just like your father.

We sang a couple of Christmas carols; I looked over at my father, he was holding his mother's hand, well, perhaps I was a bit like him; I wanted to kiss my mother's hand, but she withdrew it: I'm going to have a serious word with your father, she said. I knew what she'd say. I knew how she'd say it. She'd stand in front of him just as she used to stand in front of me, she would stand on tiptoe, as if ready to spring, she would raise her voice and spit the words out: The boy's been drinking. He wanted boxing gloves for Christmas, he's becoming just like his father, like you, she'd say, perhaps she'd shed a few tears. It would confuse him. Don't you love me? he might say. I didn't know what he'd say, but that was the gist of all our questions to her: didn't she love us? This was the element of despair in our love for her: Why did she want us to be other than what we were?

We loved her, my father and I, each in our own way, maybe we loved her in the same way, with the same desperation, the same uncertainty. Who did she want us to be? Why did she want to change us, my father did everything for her, he did everything he thought she expected of him, he did his best. He did what she told him to do, but what was it she wanted? What was it that made her difficult and disgruntled; who did she want to be, we never understood her, my father and I. We loved her but didn't understand her, and perhaps it was the same for her; she loved but couldn't understand us, there was a hole in the middle of the family, a chasm or a distance: maybe it was the distance between Torgallmenningen and Michael Krohnsgate? Perhaps it was the distance between two addresses that formed a great hole in the middle of our small family, which divided us, my father and me on one side, my mother on the other, as if we'd brought the distance between Torgallmenningen and Michael Krohnsgate with us when we moved into the house in Øyjordsveien; a distance or chasm that moved in with the family, into the house, and later into me, who didn't know where I belonged or who I was.

When the guests had finally gone, she went up to the bathroom and undressed. She took off her dress and jewellery, washed off the make-up and undid the hairpiece, pulled off her shoes and stockings; she came down the stairs in a white nightdress. She sat on the sofa and lit a cigarette; she was so different, so undressed and beautiful, pure, white, transparent, so relaxed and naked, the naked face, her mouth and nose, throat and shoulders, arms, hands, those long fingers, without rings, the nails, without nail polish, it was as if she'd divested herself of all care, all expectation, as if she'd resigned, given herself up; she wasn't angry, she sat on the sofa watching my father and me talking. It was one of those moments of happiness that suddenly came when she gave way to something strange and still, something larger than herself, a wisdom or certainty about something in the future, something unavoidable, that she couldn't oppose or alter. We would have to manage on our own, without her. We would sit by ourselves, undisturbed, but this evening, Christmas Eve, she was absent for only a few minutes, she sat on the sofa, silent, as if watching us from another place, as if she'd already left us, but then she realized that I was crying, I don't know if it was from happiness or something else, I was crying, and it irritated her: The boy's not himself, she said, he'd better go to bed.

I liked sitting in my room and smoking cigarettes out of the window. I stole cigarettes from my mother, spirits from my father; raided his bottles and then refilled them carefully with water, it was his own method, he did the same, refilled the bottles with water so that my mother wouldn't see he'd been drinking. It was a strange thing, the way he produced all this moonshine while at the same time concealing, or trying to conceal the fact that he drank it. The apparatus was in the basement, in the utility room, a large metal kettle, standing on an electric ring. A long, arched tube ran from the kettle to a flask where the alcohol was cooled and purified, ninety-six per cent. My father was a chemist; I don't believe he ever used his training for anything other than making this liquor: The best, the absolute purest spirit there is, he said. So there were two of us in the house indulging in secrets, or lies; I sat in my room with the window open, drinking moonshine which I'd watered down with orange juice, smoking cigarettes and dreaming of becoming an author. Where had I got this idea from? I'd already read quite a number of books, and occasionally, not very often, but now and then, I thought I could have written the book I'd just read.

Not the books of Doris Lessing, and never those of
Dickens or Thomas Hardy, they were impossible, and
would always remain so, I realized that as a sixteen-
or seventeen-year-old, but the books of Mykle and
Bjørneboe, they were possible to imitate, I believed,
thought. This was my own kind of foolishness but we
must be foolish in order to become writers, I know
that now but I didn't know it then: how foolish and
ignorant I was, how foolish and ignorant one had to
be to become a writer. I wanted to write books, or at
least a book, it wasn't impossible surely, books were
around, and someone must have written them. I'd just
finished *Tess of the d'Urbervilles* by Thomas Hardy, and
I felt a kinship with Tess; the girl who discovered that
she belonged to a finer and genteeler family than the
poverty-stricken one into which she'd been born. Her
parents sent her away so that she could assume her
rightful place among more elevated folk, and this
destroyed Tess, she was broken by this removal from
one place to another, I thought. The move from Skytterveien to Øyjordsveien had lost me my friends, and
I wasn't interested in trying to make new ones, not in
Øyjordsveien; it had become an impossible place for
me; we hadn't moved far enough away for me to begin

again, I couldn't create a new life here, only a few hundred yards from the blocks of Skytterveien, right under the eyes, so to speak, of the whole of Skytterveien; they would see that I'd been one boy yesterday and another today, they'd see that I was false.

Above all, I was alone; it's difficult to write the word lonely but I was lonely, I wasn't lonely: I sat in my room alone and filled page after page of diary. Diary after diary; I filled the pages with thoughts and dreams, little narratives and notes. I filled the diaries with friends male and female, girls and romances, travels and towns, places and people, and gradually as I wrote, these places and people took on a life, a life of their own; I can't say they came alive, or became real, but sometimes I dreamt about them, as if they existed, and in their own way they did; like ghosts, almost, or marionettes: some of which could have existed, or used to exist; in the same way as characters in a novel. The diaries increasingly took on the aspect of novels; I got a grasp of style, my style took shape, and from this shape could be formed, just as we form figures out of clay, or earth, hands and feet, bodies and faces, sentences and words, they seemed believable.

I achieved, through all this writing, an age that wasn't my own. I had experiences I was too young to have; I found a style, and in that style reposed everything I didn't know anything about; it popped up, appeared, took shape, I can't put it any other way; you need to have been alone a lot, I think, to be able to write what I've just described.

Tess's parents and Martha Quest's parents and my parents, perhaps all parents; they were all guilty of the same crime, they didn't know their own children. They didn't understand them, didn't know what they had inside them, they didn't see them for what they were; parents tried to force their children, who were becoming independent, wilful and free, to grow to be like them; trapped, trapped in a job or profession, in a meaningless life, I wrote in my diary as a seventeen-year-old, after reading *Tess of the d'Urbervilles*. I don't feel the same today; after twenty years as an author, and as a father, I think as my parents did before me, and perhaps as all parents do, that the best thing for my daughter would be an education and then a job. Now I'm trying to turn writing into a living; I think of writing as a job, work, I'm working to earn money, trying as best I can to provide for myself and my daughter. Even that first typewriter gave me the instantaneous feeling of work; I really was sitting in front of a machine. Each time my fingers hovered above the keyboard and pressed the keys down, letters were impressed on the white paper in small, black type. I was producing words. From where I sat at the machine I produced sentences and text, one could hear the sound of the machine stamping, not so different to the noise I'd heard from the looms in the textile factory where my father worked. I'd been given the typewriter by my mother, all that remained was to feed the first sheet of paper into the carriage and bash away. It didn't matter very much what I wrote; at first my fascination was with the sentences and words being hammered on to the page, the actual print; the printing of black characters on that whiteness.

There was an immediate rapport, or harmony, between the machine and me. As if I'd found my tool, or instrument, perhaps I was like the child who sits down at a piano and picks out its first tunes, yes, like when your internal music, the music that still hasn't found its expression, finds its instrument; I had

a strong feeling, as soon as I sat down at the typewriter, that I was doing something right; I'd found my
machine.

Not only had I found my machine but I'd also found
my place. I liked sitting at the writing table, concentrated and undisturbed, as if waiting for something I
didn't know about, hour after hour, during the
evenings and at night, a sort of alertness and concen-
tration that manifested itself in sentences and words,
often strange, sometimes unpleasant, as if they hadn't
been written by me but by someone else; I didn't
always know where these words came from. I had as
yet no credentials to make me a writer; all I had was the
ability to work, to sit still, day after day, at my writing
table. I had found my place. I had found my machine.
It would be a long time before I found the style I
needed. I knew I had to work my way towards it, the
style I needed but as yet didn't have, write towards it,
work towards it, there were no alternatives. Style
wouldn't come of its own accord. I could read books
of course, and I did, but that reading was pointless,
wasted, if it wasn't harnessed to my own writing. At
the age of seventeen I wrote my first novel. A year

later I wrote another, and at nineteen I wrote a collection of poetry: *The Chinese Puzzle*. Nothing in any of these had literary merit, and nothing in these books hinted that he who wrote them might become an author. But I was absorbed by something else: the growing stack of paper on the table. I'd written more than five hundred pages, and the pile of paper was increasing, it got thicker, taller, and I was continually laying new sheets on top of the massive heap. The stack was on the right-hand side of the typewriter; I could just sit there and look at it, perhaps it was more than two inches high; the pages were closely typed, dog-eared, smeared with bits of food and smudged with fingermarks; I thought the pages were beautiful. When I held a sheet up to the desk lamp, I could see the black lines running across it with their crossings-out and corrections. The pages had additions in handwriting, insertions between the lines and in the margin; this handwriting between the printed sentences and all the emphatic crossings-out with a pen: I found them beautiful. The content might be worthless, I would realize this only a few days later, when I read what I'd written; I'd be ashamed, angry at my incompetence, immaturity, stupidity, lack of expression, embarrassing

ideas, unnecessary descriptions, all the long mono-
logues and dreadful dialogue; I only had to read a novel
by Hamsun or Lawrence, only to compare, and I could
immediately see that what I was writing was unusable.

But by my own internal measure, that thick slab
of paper outweighed its own unreadable contents;
outweighed each detached page of unemployable
sentences. The great pile outweighed all the small,
unsuccessful words, the inconsequential, superficial
sentences; I had to go on writing.

The mound of paper lay beneath the desk lamp. The
writing table was by my bedroom window; I'd fixed
up a hook to secure my door with. I could write what
I wanted. My notes lay strewn across the table and on
the floor, in the bed and on the chairs; I wrote on
loose sheets and in notebooks, on drawing pads and
letter paper, in schoolbooks and on calendars, in a
rapid, almost illegible hand which I typed out on the
typewriter. The pile of paper grew. It seemed as if
it could grow endlessly, back then, as a sixteen- or
nineteen-year-old, I felt no limitations, the sentences
came of their own accord, the words continued to run
like a machine, a language machine that printed my

sentences and words in an even tempo, a fixed rhythm, day and night.

School during the day, writing in the evening. Schoolwork and writing; in June I left sixth-form college, three years at Bergen Katedralskole, on the science course. Three meaningless years of mathematics, biology, chemistry and physics. Those three years were meaningless but not wasted; all the classes in mathematics and chemistry had made it clear that I'd never work with figures and formulae.

I took a summer job in the textile factory where my father was a manager; I cleaned and greased looms and machines. When it closed down for the holidays I travelled to Copenhagen with a friend, he wanted to study philosophy. We decided to go back home and apply for university, get a student loan and return to Copenhagen as quickly as possible. I wrote my first novel in Copenhagen. After three major revisions and almost four years of work it was ready; by then I was twenty-three and ready to travel home from Copenhagen. I was to marry. I was to marry Eli whom I'd been with since I was seventeen and she sixteen. We'd parted when I moved to Copenhagen, now we both wanted to make a serious attempt to live together;

she'd bought a flat and furnished it, it was waiting for me, she wrote. The furniture and the living room and the double bed, it was all waiting for me, she had almost everything, she wrote, a good job and a lovely flat, it had a view of the sea, a bright living room, a small kitchen and a large bedroom leading to an additional workroom that was empty, she had everything, she wrote, except the most important thing, she needed me, she wrote, and I decided to leave Copenhagen.

I'd been allocated a room in a student hostel outside the city, Room 452, Rebæk Søpark, at Rødovre; I stood clutching the key, unlocked the door and discovered that the room was occupied. There were writing things on the desk. Course books on the floor. Shoes and jackets in the wardrobe. Underwear in the chest of drawers, make-up in the bathroom, what should I do? I went through her things. She'd packed most of her belongings in cardboard boxes, cups and dishes, letters and books, knick-knacks and a collection of dolls: clowns and toy dolls, how old was she? I was about to tell the caretaker but decided against it; I would wait for her. I showered and unpacked a few of my things, the typewriter and the pile of paper, I hadn't brought a lot from home, books and clothes, shoes and washing things, nothing more. In the evening there was to be a welcome party for the new students, a long table had been laid; I got dressed and suddenly I felt uneasy, perhaps I'd got something wrong. It was my room, I had the key and the lease, Room 452, it all fitted, except that someone was living in the room. I went out, leaving my things there, shut the door behind me and took the lift down, walked the short distance to the shopping centre where there was a bodega. A little room in which men and women sat drinking. Dark brown walls, lamps that shed almost no light, wooden tables and chairs, ashtrays and mirrors; a good place to write, I thought. When I got back to my room, she was there. The door was open, I knocked and she came and stood in the doorway. She was exactly the same height as I was. Our hair was the same colour, we had the same pale skin; I dropped my gaze. I'm sorry, she said. It's your room. I didn't know when you were coming, who was coming, if anyone was coming at all, sometimes these rooms are left empty, I'm squatting here, it's pretty common, quite a few of us do it, we live here while the rooms are empty, and move out when the new occupant arrives.

She stood in the doorway.

I didn't know what to say. May I come in? I asked. Sorry, she said. It's your room. I've lived here for three years. I've finished college and I've got a job but I haven't found a place to live. I'll move back home, she said. I don't want to but I'll go back home, to Mum or Dad, they're divorced, she said. She sat on the edge of the bed, I sat in the only chair. She had long, light brown hair tied in a ponytail. Blue eyes. Thick lips, a thin, yellow jumper, blue jeans; I found it hard to look at her. What's your name, where are you from? she asked. I told her, and she made a small movement with her head, a little toss of the head, at the same time she pressed her forefinger to her lower lip, a soft pressure of nail against mouth; it was as if I recognized that movement. She sat on the edge of the bed, I sat in the only chair; it was as if that motion of the head, as if the whole strange situation in this room that was neither hers nor mine, was predetermined, as if I'd known of the whole thing previously and recognized it all, as if, without knowing it, I'd been waiting for this moment and knew it as soon as she pressed her finger to her lip. In that instant I knew precisely what would happen, it struck me like some preordained bolt of lightning, we'd both live in the room.

I moved in, she didn't move out. The idea was that she'd move out, as soon as she found a flat in Copenhagen, but she stayed on. She stayed on provided I undertook to make no advances whatsoever, she brought me to an agreement: I wouldn't touch her, she wouldn't look at any of my papers. It didn't take us long to adjust to the small room; she slept in the bed, I slept on a mattress on the floor. She got up early and cycled to the job she'd found in a clothes shop, I sat at the desk, working until she got home. It was a kind of double joy, I was happy to be alone, to have the whole day to myself, and I looked forward to her return to the little room; I waited for her.

All of a sudden, and without any effort except moving, from Bergen to Copenhagen, to Rødovre, that suburb of residential blocks and green spaces, I was happy. It was as if I'd moved back to where I came from, I'd come home. The sun shone through the window. There was a spray of white chrysanthemums on the desk. The sun filled the room with summer, with autumn. Students played football on the pitch between the blocks, I could see them from my window; behind the football field a stream fed a pond with ducks and geese, where girls lay in a ring round the water studying in the sun. I wrote from ten till one, had lunch in the communal kitchen, and then went for a walk through the park and into the woods; paths fanned out in all directions, but I always went the same way, through the wood and out to the beach where I stripped off and swam. Twice a week, on Tuesdays and Thursdays, I cycled to lectures at the Institute of Art History, these were held in an old warehouse near Copenhagen's Langelinie; I cycled into the courtyard and took the stairs to the second floor; here Teddy Brunius would lecture on Anders Zorn, or Edvard Munch, he lectured on nineteenth-century Scandinavian art, a squat, square man in a dark suit and white shirt and sporting a broad, black tie that made him look as if he came from the era he was discussing; for a few hours he managed to transport us back in time, for a few hours we were, with Teddy Brunius, contemporaries of Søren Kierkegaard and Hans Christian Andersen. My writing was more focused than ever before, I wanted to write a novel. I sat at my desk from ten to one, had a break and then wrote from three until Linda came back from her job around five. We ate dinner together, and spent the evenings in the TV lounge, or she would lie on her bed and talk away, she loved talking; there was so much she wanted to say, so much she wanted to tell. One evening she said: I'm going out tonight. I'm meeting someone, I'm not sure if I'll be home. You mustn't wait up for me. I lay there waiting for her. I hoped and thought that she'd be back, it was a dangerous game, I almost jumped up and ran out to look for her, but where, I didn't know Copenhagen, any of the nightspots; I'd been shut up with her.

She returned at last. It was early morning, I heard her at the door; she walked straight over to the corner where I lay on the floor with my eyes closed, stood above me and took off her clothes, jacket and boots, she stood over me in her see-through blouse and short, black skirt; I could see her pubic hair, her naked sex under her skirt, she bent over me: Are you asleep? she asked. You mustn't try to make me unhappy, I said. She lay down on the bed, on a synthetic animal skin she had, lay semi-naked on the animal skin and propped her head up on her right arm: I'm doing it for your sake, she said. I don't need it, I said. But your book does, she said.

I called her Louise in the book. I moved the action to another city, altered her appearance and reworked the stories she told into a novel. I wrote it during the day while Linda was at work, and at night when she'd gone to sleep; I sat at the desk writing longhand at night. A special stillness and joy at night; I draped a white shirt over the desk lamp, sat in the half-darkness and looked out of the window at the row of blocks and the windows on the other side of the lawn; I imagined us living in one of those rooms. A small room with two lamps and a desk, a narrow bed and two people pacing back and forth in the little room, like captives, captive, I could envisage them as shadows or silhouettes, a young woman and man, exactly the same height, who resembled each other. I wanted them to resemble each other. I wanted them to be precisely the same age, she was nineteen and born in November, he'd been born in the same month. They didn't know each other, didn't love each other, they lived together in a small room; I wanted them to be like two characters in a novel.

At the weekends they cycled out to the beach. It was late August, the sun was still hot, the sea warm; we swam and lay side by side on the sand.

They cycled up the beach road to Humlebæk and Louisiana to see Giacometti's sculptures, the tall, thin male figure walking, the tall, thin female figure standing; they stood next to the sculptures and measured, she was exactly the same height as the female figure and he was the same height as the male figure. They took pictures of each other and pasted them up on the wall of the room they lived in: she was striding out in the picture, one leg in front of the other, he stood straight with his arms by his sides.

We must do it differently, she said.

We cycled up the beach road to see Karen Blixen's house. A large, white house with a rose garden, the flowers climbing red, yellow up the white brick wall, up towards the windows that their vigorous petals almost covered and closed. Behind the house; another garden, or a park with paths and trees, beech, aspen, ash, birch and chestnut, a fish pond and herb garden, countless birdboxes in the trees, to protect the

female birds and their eggs. A slight rise where Karen
Blixen lay buried beneath a tree. She sat at the desk in
her study, a mahogany escritoire, a chair made of
cedar, an African rug under the desk and heavy
curtains that ran down the wall and a little way across
the floor, as if she wished to prolong her life; a curtain material that she'd stretched out and wrapped
around herself in a kind of dress, around her legs and
hips and up over her body and stomach and breast,
around her throat and mouth, a thin, yellowish-white
material over her nose and eyes, over her ears in a tur-
ban that covered her hair and hid her face in a new
and terrible attire; it bound her tight to the desk as if
she were a flower. She sat at her desk encased in yellow curtain fabric which was wrapped around her in
leaves. We cycled past the house, past the rose garden
and windows, along Strandveien and back to Copenhagen; towards the lights that flared up out of the half
darkness, red, yellow, white, a special blue above the
housetops, over the city, an autumnal blue sky, over
the streets, those grey blocks of brick that lay in pon-
derous rows towards the city centre where the streets
opened and got lighter. We cycled past nightspots and
cafes, dance clubs and restaurants, parked our bikes

and walked down Skindergade to Krasnapolsky. The place was full, crammed with people around the square bar. A packed dance floor at the back, loud music, flashes of light and hands, bodies and heads, we pushed our way in. Pushed our way into the soft mass, the pungent scent of perfume and sweat, slid into a gentle network of touch and glance, it was impossible to tell one face from another, we were all alike, all, apart from one; he stood with his back to the wall wearing white trousers, braces over a shiny, blue shirt open at the neck. His chalk white neck supported a round head with large, dark eyes that stared out from two black holes of make-up smeared across his face beneath the sparse, white hair that stood erect, stiff with hair gel. It was Poul Borum. He looked like a bird. A large, heavy bird; he stood erect and didn't move. He stood with his back to the wall staring wildly out at the floor where we were moving in a slow circle round the bar and in towards the dance floor where we danced. We danced and winter was on the way. There were snowflakes in the sky, white and airy, they danced in the darkness and melted in the street, the black asphalt that turned white with rime and frost at night. In December I read one of Poul Borum's books, I read it carefully, over and over. It was the first time I'd read a book to learn something about it, to study the book's secrets and techniques, to examine how it was written and assembled. I wanted to look at the language of its poetry. How it could impart something in a more complex way, a more concentrated way, a deeper and truer way, perhaps, I wasn't sure, didn't understand everything I read, but the book concerned me very deeply; I began to read poetry.

I read all of Poul Borum's books and the books of Inger Christensen and several of Klaus Høeck's books, I read Søren Ulrik Thomsen's books and Michael Strunge's books, F. P. Jac's books and Pia Tafdrup's book, I read Terje Dragseth's books, and these books of poetry changed my style; I wanted to write novels as if they were poetry. There was so much I wanted, so much I couldn't manage: One day, it was in early April, Linda planted herself in my chair at the writing table, well wrapped up and with a cap on, as if she'd planned to leave in a hurry, she seemed agitated, she must be moving, I thought, she's found a place to live. This book of yours, she said. This crappy book of yours is full of lies and mistakes, you lie and tell everything the wrong way, you lie and your book isn't genuine, she shouted. It makes me sick to read it, you make me sick, she hissed. You must write your book again, I insist on it, she said. I insist that you write it all over again, properly, without lying, without being false. You're not supposed to read my stuff, we had an agreement, I said. I don't give a toss about agreements, she said, you're writing about me and it's my book, I've given it to you and what you put down must be correct, don't you understand how important that is? she asked. It's a novel, I said. I'm not an idiot, she screamed. I know perfectly well it's a novel but what you've written isn't true, your novel is false, she yelled. You make me stupider than I am, weaker than I am, falser than I am, you make us both stupider and falser than we are, you make us smaller than we are, and if it had been a real novel it would have made us bigger than we are.

The sun struck her face. She pulled a pair of sunglasses out of her bag, slid them in front of her eyes: You don't know me, she said.

I've never had a boyfriend. I've never been with anyone, never loved anyone, I've always been alone, she said. I never wanted to be alone, I wanted to be with

someone, have a lover, perhaps I wanted it too much,
I've never met anyone, anyone I liked better than myself, that I liked enough to want to be with. I'm telling
you this because I'm moving out. When you stood in
the doorway, I thought you were like me. I wanted to
give it a try, take a chance, I thought we suited each
other but I can't live here with you when you write the
way you do, you're ruining things for us, she said. She
pressed her forefinger to her lower lip. In that instant
I could see how she'd get up and leave the room. I
rose quickly and wanted to go to her and hold her
tight. I wanted to put my arms around her and make
love to her and be with her and do everything I could
not to lose her but I just stood there bolt upright and
couldn't raise my arms, they were pinned down by a
strange certainty: it was necessary for her to move out.
I'd already written about it in the novel: how she
walked from the room with long, quick strides, how I
was left in the middle of the room with my arms
hanging by my sides.

I was alone in the room, Room 452, the little room
had suddenly become too big, and it was painful to
live there; I wanted to change rooms, move to one in

a different block, a different floor, but it was impossible, I had to stay in the room. Last year, I was on a reading tour in Denmark, I took the train from Copenhagen's central station to the college in Rødovre; I got off the train and couldn't remember whether to turn right or left but eventually found the subway leading to the rows of residential blocks behind the shopping centre; where was the block I'd lived in? I walked up and down, crossed the park in various directions and finally found the block and the room, number 452, someone had attempted to break into the room and the door had been kicked to pieces. I stood there for a long time gazing at the ruined door; it aroused no emotions in me, no pain or pleasure, just confusion; had I lived here? I could, at any time, have taken the train into town and seen Linda at the shop where she worked; I could have said that I was sorry, that I'd do anything for her, that I'd alter the book to make her happy, I could have asked her to move back in, begged her, we could move to a place in town, a bigger place, a flat with several rooms, I wanted to ask her, but I didn't do it; I stayed on alone in the room, it was painful to live there. And perhaps it was this loss, this almost unendurable longing, this terrible hurt, that is now completely vanished and irretrievable, like a wound that heals and turns into a scar that becomes part of the skin, you can't find it anywhere on your body, this wound that once was so painful that you'd never have believed such pain was possible, it disappears among other wounds and larger scars, but perhaps it was precisely this first wound that enabled me to write a novel at last.

The novel was published, two years later, in September; I got a copy in the post. By then I'd drafted the book four times, each time with a typewriter, page by page, I'd written more than a thousand pages, I'd cut and inserted, corrected and rewritten, I worked harder on that book than on any other. That first copy: I collected it from the post office at Rødovre. I opened the packet and put the book into my jacket pocket, took the train into Copenhagen and walked about the streets with the novel in my pocket. I was an author. I wasn't an author yet but I walked about the streets of Copenhagen and told myself I was an author, I had the proof in my pocket, the novel, of course it proved nothing, but on that day, that first day with that first book in my jacket pocket, I was an author.

I walked around Copenhagen behaving like an author, the way I thought that an author should behave; in the evenings I went to Cafe Dan Turèll and drank beer and smoked cigarettes, before going on to Cafe Sommersko, and later to Bo Bi Bar, and afterwards to Andy's Bar where I stayed until closing time, night after night, morning after morning. It was time to go home. I took the bus to Rødovre, packed my few belongings into two boxes and dispatched the boxes by train to Bergen.

So I moved from Rødovre to Eli's flat in Bergen's Kirkegaten. A few days previously I'd had practically nothing, now I'd got almost everything; we had a large living room with a dining table and six chairs, two sofas and a coffee table, lamps and a bookshelf, we had a bright bedroom with a large double bed and a white, shaggy carpet, we had a dishwasher and a fridge and a brand new cooker, the kitchen looked out over the city and the sea. I was allotted a small workroom leading off the bedroom, where I sat and dozed. I sat in there and couldn't produce anything, not even one decent page, not even a reasonable sentence; the right words wouldn't come, I couldn't find them, and after a few days in Kirkegaten I came to a complete stand-still, I was unable to write, all was silence. I tried various tricks; I took my notebooks to a cafe, tried to write in various places in town. I got up in the middle of the night, tried to write at night or early in the morning, drank a bottle of wine or spirits, tried to write while I was drunk or hung over, I sat in the living room and in the kitchen but the right words didn't come, the sentences weren't good enough, not necessary enough, and finally I gave up, I couldn't write; I was no longer an author.

I didn't know how to occupy my time; I sat at my writing table and waited for Eli to return from her job in a boutique. We ate dinner together, in the evenings we sat on the sofa and watched television, or we went to bed early: one morning, it was a Sunday, we were lying in bed devoid of plans, we didn't know what to do or where we were going, we lay in bed not knowing how we should pass the time, a perfectly ordinary Sunday in December, just before Christmas, we'd talked about getting married; it was snowing, a fine, cold snow that covered the streets, it felt as if they would disappear, the streets and houses, as if the streets and the houses and the whole city was disappearing beneath a white blanket of snow, we were lying in bed and looking at the snow which covered the windowsill and half the pane, when one of us, I can't remember which, but one of us must have said: This is no good.

I got out of bed and dressed; we didn't argue, neither of us blamed the other for anything, we hugged each other and agreed that I would collect my things one day the following week; my father would help me with a van from the factory. We'd move my boxes from Kirkegaten to Øyjordsveien. Then I walked out of the door, down the stairs from the fourth floor of the block, trudged out into the snow; I turned left into Amalie Skramsvei, strode off, all the way home to my boyhood bedroom in Øyjordsveien.

I don't know precisely when old age arrives, when it manifests itself; at a certain point we lose the ability to determine our own age, we get younger and younger with the years, or it may be that we become stuck in a variety of ages, that we are thoroughly nineteen and thirty and fifty-seven, all at once, no longer is there one age but several; it's an imperceptible transition from truth to invention, we make up our age and name, who we are and who we want to be.

There are so many possibilities, so many names and places, we've gathered them up and can't distinguish between them with the same clarity as before. We live one life and then another, and after that a new one, and just as with the idea of transmigration, we register that something from a former life has accompanied us into the new one; some faces, some names, that's all we remember.

We are setting out on a new life, in a new room at a new address, without parents, without a lover; perhaps you're living alone with a child, a teenager, it won't be long before she's grown up. It won't be long before she moves out, until you lose yourself entirely.

I move to a place I've never been before.

I go home.

A new book; a strange place.

A new book; a new home, uninhabitable, as always.

I go home to a place I've never been before.

Perhaps it's when you're at home that you're most a stranger.

I have constructed a woman's body; an apron, women's clothes, hairpieces and eye shadow; I've inherited my mother's clothes and my mother's things from my father.

Marte Huke writes: In the mornings I have to break into my clothes.

In the mornings I have to break into my clothes, they're too tight, they're too small. I can hardly get my jacket on. My shirt, trousers, shoes and jacket, my clothes, they don't want to do the same thing as me.

The way the voice gets higher. The throat seems tighter. The tongue narrower. The mouth wider, a higher, more powerful voice, I can call my daughter with it.

Even the eyes alter. I don't see the same things.

The hair, the nails, grow. The legs stretch. Strides get longer, a swinging gait.

It won't be long before I have to tie my hair back when I run.

The bedroom, blue. An ice-cold, light blue wallpaper with silver lilies embossed on the thick material. An English wallpaper with ice flowers, half open, as if flowering in the cold, as if Nature has been inverted and is following artificial laws: plastic flowers in a vase on the bedside table. A double bed with a brown bedspread. White pillows, white duvet, white sheets; a sudden feeling of happiness, of freedom, of nothing.

Brown, thick curtains: it's best when they're drawn in towards the middle, the middle of the window, a small opening in the middle, a narrow strip of light, a September-strip or an April-gash, as when you plunge a knife into trouser material and rip.

Sleep changes too: I sleep more lightly, wake more often, as if my hearing has become more acute, or are my ears sticking out in a different way?

A new ear, growing out of the old one.

As if the skin is wax and is creased into new shapes, bags of skin that are filled with weight and fat in new places. As if sleep stretches the skin out and folds it up again in novel ways; a new body, it covers the old one, the sleeping posture has had to change.

The dreams are new too. I'm sleeping in a white nightdress.

The light is switched on, it's not enough, you open the curtains, turn all the lamps on, it gets no lighter.

My name is spoken, repeatedly, it isn't the right name.

A pointed, humanoid face with wings, settles on the chest and draws the breath out of the sleeper. A pleasant cold, protective and warm; I want to wake up but I can't.

The rooms, too, are altered. The bedroom has a window overlooking the sea. Askøy lies on the other side of the fjord like an embankment against the sea; the island and the clouds, the heavy covering of cloud, silver and grey, block off the sea and the light, as if the island casts shadows through the bedroom window.

As if the oak tree in front of the house is growing in through the window and spreading its branches in the bedroom; I'm sleeping on the top of a tree. Its leaves curl, change colour and fall off the branches, there are acorns on the floor at the foot of the bed.

My style will alter as well, gradually, as when we exchange one name for another, one sentence for a new one, that first sentence, it must be soft as wax.

That first sentence, we work it up, fetch and gather the words we find and cement them together with other words, a sticky lump of words, soft. We work up a structure, a cube, almost, which we fill with words: the patterns are formed, the sentence shines.

That first sentence must be soft. What we have in common, my daughter and I, is that we both miss our mothers. We have breakfast together in the kitchen, it's early in the morning, she's due at school by half past eight, it takes almost an hour by bus to Olsvik where her school is, roughly halfway between Øyjordsveien and Ask; she inhabits two worlds, she's kept the friends she had from Askøy and has made some new ones in Øyjordsveien. She travels backwards and forwards between two places; I try to remain static in one, I hardly move around.

I don't want to.

I move about the house, it has three storeys. A basement room, an in-between storey with living room and kitchen, our bedrooms are at the top of the house.

I go up and down the stairs of the house.

I don't know why but I love these stairs; going up and down the treads, sitting on the steps, I've put a bed under the basement stairs and sleep there when I need a change, or when I can't sleep, when I'm scared and wakeful and need shelter.

Like sleeping in a nest, in a hole, in a hole in the ground.

Sometimes I sleep like an animal, at others I sleep like a mother.

I lie waiting, listening, even in sleep I wait for her to come home.

Even in sleep I can hear her, even though she's not there.

We have breakfast, I make her packed lunch and she races out of the door, off to the bus. I sit down on the stairs, in my mother's spot, light a cigarette and smoke like she did. Sometimes I use my mother's voice; I say the same things to my daughter as my mother said to me, I say: Now go and tidy your room. Don't be home too late. This house does have rules, you know.

The rules of the house; I follow them.

Once a day, just before dinner, I go down to the shop, I need to buy milk and bread and cigarettes. I need to buy stuff for breakfast and dinner and supper. After dinner I tidy the house, hoover and wash up. I wash our sheets and clothes, hanging them on the clothes line outside, when it isn't raining.

The smell of newly washed clothes; I breathe it in.

The smell of coats hanging in the hall; I press my nose deep into the material and see her in my mind's eye.

Today I washed the living room windows; I went out and peered in, I went in and looked out, it was a minor event, a great joy.

Outside the house: you imagine the people who live inside.

We live in a terraced house, I'm fond of our neighbours, a youngish couple in the house on the left, an elderly couple in the house on the right; I don't think we're either better or worse off than them.

I like the sounds they make, neighbourly noises; I hear them going up and down the stairs. The couple in the house on the right are pensioners and have been married for almost forty years, they spend most of the summer sitting on the patio, under the awning, where they've got a patio heater, they listen to the radio and talk quietly, I hear her laughing at something he says, I can hear that they still love each other.

The young couple on the left have got a cat, a silvery-white Forest cat, it creeps under the garden fence and lies in a particular spot in my garden, in a little hollow it's made beneath the oleaster, it's a beautiful cat; as soon as I see it crawling under the fence, I start up from my chair and run into the garden and chase it away.

I make dinner each day, each day I buy and cook the food; I remember how my mother complained: It'll drive me mad, she'd say, having to think of things for dinner every single day, Monday, Tuesday, Wednesday and Thursday, Friday and Saturday and Sunday, make something for dinner, its driving me mad wondering what to make for dinner today and tomorrow and the next day, every blessed day having to think of what we'll eat for dinner, it's driving me round the bend, she'd say, and it was awful to listen to, awful to think about, I found it awful to think that every day she had to think up something to make that we could eat for dinner.

Every day we have dinner together, my daughter and I. Once a week my father joins us for a meal; I make something with potatoes, fish or meat, always with potatoes: This is the only time in the week I eat potatoes, my father says. Don't you have dinner every day? I ask. No, he says.

After dinner my father and I have coffee, we sit in the living room looking out of the window, at the ships sailing in and out of the harbour; out beneath the bridges and out of the estuary towards the skerries and the open sea. It's a fine view, says my father. You must have dinner every day, I tell him. Every day you must go for a walk. It's important that you eat and take a walk, every single day, I tell him.

On Sundays we go to watch football, the ground is just across the road from the sheltered housing where he lives; I ring at the main door downstairs, seethe over the time it takes my father to come down, that he takes the lift and not the stairs, it irritates me that he's begun to get old. At last he arrives, we cross the road and go through the gates, pay for our tickets and take our seats on the stand. It's Sandviken against Stabæk. Women's Premier League. Just think when I was chairman of Sandviken I voted against women's football, my father says. We have a good laugh at this. We sit on the stand and laugh: I suppose basically, I've always made the wrong choices, says my father.

On Saturdays I cycle into town and buy the papers. I settle in a cafe, always the same cafe, always in the same seat, by the window. A large window with a view of Olav Kyrresgate and the trees in the park and the mountains behind. I order a croissant and a coffee, which is brought to my table by a man. He wears black trousers, a black shirt and a white apron. He has an unnaturally high voice, disturbing. When you've renounced love, you can end up loving anyone at all.

While I'm in town, I've got to do some household shopping; we need hoover bags and Plumbo for the drains. We need toiletries and cosmetics, hair dye and creams, soap and shampoos, balm and a new hair dryer. My daughter needs new clothes, I buy a pink down jacket and two pairs of jeans (she wants to change them), a pair of wellies (she wants to change them) and a pair of white tennis shoes, a pair of blue Nike track pants and a silver Puma shoulder bag. I go to the bookshop and buy a Danish edition of Ovid's *Metamorphoses*. At the bookshop I buy what stationery I need, printing ribbons and correcting ribbons for the typewriter, two biros, correcting fluid and four notebooks. It's always hard to begin a new book. I buy a packet of five hundred sheets of typing paper, a new pair of scissors, two reels of clear tape, a glue-stick and some pencils. Then I cycle home, as fast as I can, it's almost three o'clock, I take the quickest route, along Bryggen and the wharves, up the gravel road through Bergenhus Fortress, out of the gate, past the Bontelabo cold-storage building and the old wharf-side warehouses. I cycle up the cobbled road towards the old town, Gamle Bergen, at top speed past the wooden houses and gardens, the duck pond and sea-baths, through the city gate and down past the residential blocks, up the hill towards the Technical

College. The lilac bushes have lost their flowers, the honeysuckle, clematises and rose bushes, are flowerless. The rowan trees have produced berries, they hang in red clusters. The season is changing; I wheel my bike up the final slopes to Øyjordsveien. It's always hard to start a new life. I steal an apple from the tree on the corner, walking more slowly now, eating the apple and halting beneath the great beech that stands at the entrance to the school garden. From here I can see the house we live in, a narrow, small timber building with steps up to each door: sometimes I just stand under the tree, not wanting to go in. Sometimes I think that we should have lived somewhere else, in a different house, that we could have lived a totally different life. But as soon as I walk up the gravel path and let myself in the door, I'm intensely glad to be home.